Affirmative Rhetoric, Negative Action:
African-American and Hispanic Faculty at Predominantly White Institutions

by Valora Washington and William Harvey

ASHE-ERIC Higher Education Report 2, 1989

Prepared by

Clearinghouse on Higher Education
The George Washington University

In cooperation with

Association for the Study
of Higher Education

Published by

School of Education and Human Development
The George Washington University

Jonathan D. Fife, Series Editor

Cite as
Washington, Valora and William Harvey. *Affirmative Rhetoric, Negative Action: African-American and Hispanic Faculty at Predominantly White Institutions.* Report No. 2. Washington, D.C.: School of Education and Human Development, The George Washington University, 1989.

Library of Congress Catalog Card Number 89-83593
ISSN 0884-0040
ISBN 0-9623882-1-1

Managing Editor: Christopher Rigaux
Cover design by Michael David Brown, Rockville, Maryland

The ERIC Clearinghouse on Higher Education invites individuals to submit proposals for writing monographs for the ASHE-ERIC Higher Education Report series. Proposals must include:
1. A detailed manuscript proposal of not more than five pages.
2. A chapter-by-chapter outline.
3. A 75-word summary to be used by several review committees for the initial screening and rating of each proposal.
4. A vita and a writing sample.

ERIC Clearinghouse on Higher Education
School of Education and Human Development
The George Washington University
One Dupont Circle, Suite 630
Washington, DC 20036-1183

This publication was prepared partially with funding from the Office of Educational Research and Improvement, U.S. Department of Education, under contract no. ED RI-88-062014. The opinions expressed in this report do not necessarily reflect the positions or policies of OERI or the Department.

EXECUTIVE SUMMARY

This is an analysis of affirmative action theory and practice for African-American and Hispanic faculty in predominantly white, four-year institutions of higher education. It examines the history of affirmative action, supply and demand issues, institutional approaches to affirmative action, factors outside of the academy that affect faculty employment, and case studies of effective practices or new initiatives.

Critics and advocates of affirmative action have focused on similar issues in debates. Both groups often assume that affirmative action has led to significant increases in the number of minority faculty at predominantly white institutions, but this is not the case. Both groups also cite the threat of federal action as a result of affirmative action failure. However, no college or university has ever lost federal funds as a result of noncompliance—or if they have, this fact has not been publicized.

Several questions for consideration emerge as we approach the 1990s. Is affirmative action really necessary? Why hasn't more progress been made in hiring African-American and Hispanic faculty? What should be done to increase employment opportunities for African-American and Hispanic faculty?

Is Affirmative Action Really Necessary?

Any discussion of affirmative action must recall the historical factors leading to this solution. Before World War II, Hispanics and African-Americans were virtually invisible in higher education. Moreover, lack of "qualified" minority faculty was not the reason for the racial segregation of faculty. Even by 1936, there was a sizable group of African-Americans with Ph.D.s, 80 percent of whom taught at three historically African-American institutions (Atlanta, Fisk, and Howard Universities). By 1941, only two African-American tenured faculty members in predominantly white institutions can be identified. By 1947, out of 3,000 African-Americans who listed "college teacher" as their occupation, only 78 had ever taught at a white school—many as part-time lecturers. By 1958 there were 200 African-American faculty members at predominantly white institutions, a figure that increased to 300 by 1961.

By 1972—the year affirmative action in higher education was initiated—African-Americans represented 2.9 percent of all faculty (including those at historically African-American universities). Other minority groups (including Hispanics, but not Asians) were 2.8 percent of the total faculty. There were only 1,500 faculty who could be identified as Mexican-American or Chicano (600 of these were at community colleges).

The number of African-American and Hispanic faculty increased until 1976, then began to level off or decline. Between 1977 and 1984, national faculty representation for African-Americans dropped from about 4.4 percent to 4.0 percent, and for Hispanics from 1.7 percent to 1.4 percent. Note that most of the African-American faculty are at historically African-American institutions (although they comprise just 60 percent of the faculty at historically African-American institutions).

Affirmative action continues to be necessary because of its limited success, and because of the pluralistic nature of our society. Colleges—as institutions where people expect to challenge their perspectives and values—can help prepare our nation to deal with diversity in many ways: by providing students with role models, by preparing minority youth to assume positions of leadership, and by supporting minority-related scholarship.

Why Hasn't More Progress Been Made in Hiring African-American and Hispanic Faculty?

Proponents of the "availability pool" rationale for the low numbers of African-American and Hispanic faculty can readily point to data to support their arguments: the small and/or declining number of African-American/Hispanic Ph.D.s; the underrepresentation of minorities in particular disciplines such as science and engineering; the concentration of African-American and Hispanic doctorates in the fields of education, humanities, and social sciences; and the trend toward non-academic employment among doctoral degree holders.

Nevertheless, the lack of affirmative action progress cannot be explained solely by arguments about the availability pool. The proportion of African-Americans and Hispanics who hold faculty positions in predominantly white institutions has never come close to the percentage of African-Americans and Hispanics who hold terminal degrees, even in fields where the supply is relatively good. Indeed, the decline of the African-American professoriat in the late 1970s occurred despite growth in the total number of faculty positions and in the number of African-Americans with Ph.D.s. In certain fields, minorities are more likely than whites to state their reason for working part time as the inability to find full-time employment.

These facts raise issues about the demand for African-American and Hispanic faculty. While it is important to increase the number of minorities with doctorates, it must be stressed that those who are already available and qualified are not being fully employed. Most minorities who have been hired have not had any special or preferential treatment.

Other reasons besides supply and demand explain the lack of progress in hiring African-American and Hispanic faculty: the lack of accurate availability data; the political and philosophical dominance of issues related to merit and qualification standards, rather than equity and fair process; the focus on regulation-compliance rather than on advocacy in affirmative action operations; and an atmosphere of "deferred responsibility" within institutions, where administrators, faculty, students, and staff each hold other groups responsible.

What Should Be Done to Increase Employment Opportunities for African-American and Hispanic Faculty?

Institutions of higher education should experience more affirmative action success if they adopt proactive, rather than reactive, approaches to seeking African-American and Hispanic faculty. Visible and determined leadership by the chief executive and academic officers of the university is the most important element that sets the stage for successful affirmative action. Strong leaders treat affirmative action as an institutional priority for resources and staff by closely monitoring decisions and offering incentives.

The role of the faculty is also critical for affirmative action in higher education, although there is little credible evidence of strong faculty commitment to it. Rather, many successful affirmative action programs are the outgrowth of leadership among members of the target groups who are already part of the campus community.

Search committees are the standard tool for screening and interviewing candidates; hence, their composition and work strategies are important. In choosing committee members, more flexibility in defining rank and subspecialties, and the use of minority networks or vitae banks may also be useful.

Effective affirmative action offices reflect the mission and purpose of their institutions. They work to set goals rather than respond to the timelines and goals set by others. Ideally, the affirmative action officer reports to the president and does not serve concurrently as chief academic officer.

New ideas and innovative approaches are needed to develop, recruit, and retain African-American and Hispanic professors. Some institutions are using curriculum review as a key to hiring (e.g., Temple University). Others build a pool of potential professors through incentives to graduate students, including financial support and mentoring (e.g., Wayne State University and the Florida Endowment Fund). Improving primary and secondary educational opportunities (e.g., Ohio State University) is a long-term strategy.

Conclusion

A window of opportunity for recruiting African-American and Hispanic faculty now exists, since one-third or more of the nation's professoriat may be replaced by the end of the century. This speaks to the urgency of working affirmatively at the early stages of schooling to ensure that minority youth will be prepared to enter the pipeline.

ADVISORY BOARD

Roger G. Baldwin
Assistant Professor of Education
College of William and Mary

Carol M. Boyer
Consultant and Senior Academic Planner
Massachusetts Board of Regents of Higher Education

Ellen Earle Chaffee
Associate Commissioner of Academic Affairs
North Dakota State Board of Higher Education

Martin Finkelstein
Associate Professor of Higher Education Administration
Seton Hall University

Carol Everly Floyd
Associate Vice Chancellor for Academic Affairs
Board of Regents of the Regency Universities System
State of Illinois

George D. Kuh
Professor of Higher Education
Indiana University

Yvonna S. Lincoln
Associate Professor of Higher Education
University of Kansas

Michael A. Olivas
Professor of Law
University of Houston

Richard F. Wilson
Associate Chancellor
University of Illinios

Ami Zusman
Principal Analyst, Academic Affairs
University of California

CONSULTING EDITORS

Robert J. Barak
Deputy Executive Secretary
Director of Academic Affairs and Research
Iowa Board of Regents

Robert Berdahl
Professor of Higher Education
University of Maryland

Kenneth A. Bruffee
Director, The Scholars Program
Brooklyn College of the City of New York

L. Leon Campbell
Provost and Vice President for Academic Affairs
University of Delaware

Charles S. Claxton
Associate Professor
Center for the Study of Higher Education
Memphis State University

Susan Cohen
Associate, Project for Collaborative Learning
Lesley College

John W. Creswell
Professor and Lilly Project Director
University of Nebraska

Andre Deruyttere
Vice President
Catholic University at Leuven, Belgium

Mary E. Dilworh
Director, Research and Information Services
ERIC Clearinghouse on Teacher Education

Irwin Feller
Director, Institute for Policy Research and Evaluation
Pennsylvania State University

Kenneth C. Green
Associate Director
Higher Education Research Institute
University of California at Los Angeles

Milton Greenberg
Provost
American University

Judith Dozier Hackman
Associate Dean
Yale University

Brian L. Hawkins
Vice President for Computing and Information Sciences
Brown University

Lynn G. Johnson
Executive Director
Hudson-Mohawk Association of Colleges and Universities

Carl J. Lange
Professor Emeritus
The George Washington University

Oscar T. Lenning
Vice President for Academic Affairs
Robert Wesleyan College

Judith B. McLaughlin
Research Associate on Education and Sociology
Harvard University

Andrew T. Masland
Judicial/Public Safety Market Manager
Digital Equipment Corporation

Richard I. Miller
Professor of Higher Education
Ohio University

James R. Mingle
Executive Director
State Higher Education Executive Officers

Elizabeth M. Nuss
Executive Director
National Association of Student Personnel Administrators

Anne M. Pratt
Director for Foundation Relations
College of William and Mary

Karen T. Romer
Associate Dean for Academic Affairs
Brown University

Mary Ellen Sheridan
Director of Sponsored Programs Administration
Ohio State University

Betty Taylor
Coordinator, Office of Educational Policy
New Jersey Department of Higher Education

J. Fredericks Volkwein
Director of Institutional Research
State University of New York at Albany

William R. Whipple
Director, Honors Program
University of Maine

Reginald Wilson
Senior Scholar
American Council on Education

CONTENTS

Tables

FOREWORD

This report is not about a failed vision, but about a vision that did not materialize. This vision of achieving parity for minorities in the ranks of professoriat has been held by many higher education leaders long before the days of Martin Luther King and the Civil Rights Movement of the 1960s. The question is why, with a vision so noble and so much a part of the basic values of the society, higher education, which exists because it represents what is basically good in our society, has not been able to bring this vision to fruition.

While the answers to this question cover a variety of conditions and reasons, the real explanation is in the failure of higher education to set in a clear, unequivocal, operational terms how its expectations were to be achieved and then to accept no deviation from this goal. Too often the leadership of higher education willingly accepted defeat rather than develop alternative strategies when desired results were not produced. Success is achieved through a passionate belief in the worth of a pursuit and unswerving persistence towards achieving that goal. This report clearly details that higher education had neither the passion nor the persistence to achieve its goal of equal minority participation.

This report, written by Valora Washington of Antioch College and William Harvey of North Carolina State University, emphasizes the need for higher education to shift from a policy of nondiscrimination to one of affirmative action. As the authors have concluded, there is a clear opportunity for higher education to take advantage of faculty positions being vacated due to retirement during the mid-to-late 1990s. Preparations can be made now to provide opportunities for minority students to enter graduate school and be prepared for a future career in the professoriat. The commitment of higher education to affirmative action will be clearly evidenced by the mid-1990's through a success or continued failure to insure the enrollment of minority students in its graduate program. This report clearly defines the issues and actions to be taken in order for affirmative rhetoric to also mean affirmative results.

Jonathan D. Fife
Professor and Director
ERIC Clearinghouse on Higher Education
School of Education and Human Development
The George Washington University

ACKNOWLEDGMENTS

Completing this manuscript required the help and good humor of many individuals. We are indebted to our families and colleagues at Antioch College and North Carolina State University for their support. Special thanks are due to the following administrative assistants at Antioch College who provided technical services: Lori Harding, Hope Harkins, John Shilson, Sue Smart, Jennifer Vorih, and Nancy Wilburn. Janine Strother, an administrative assistant at Antioch College, put forth commendable effort in both the manuscript revisions and in coordinating our long-distance collaboration. The following Antioch College faculty and administrators also provided useful assistance in data collection: Michael Anderson, Jewel Graham, Oliver Loud, Nina Myatt, and Betty Pettiford.

AN OVERVIEW OF AFFIRMATIVE ACTION FOR AFRICAN-AMERICAN AND HISPANIC FACULTY

To observe the American culture is to be struck by not only its accomplishments, but also its contradictions. The growth and development of the country are in some ways unparalleled in recorded history, but in other ways, for example in situations that have a racial dimension, the nation's stated values and beliefs are frequently confounded by its policies and practices.

Affirmative action brings to the surface some of the paradoxical aspects of our national experience.

The national complexities and contradictions have been the subject of observation by numerous scholars, both African-American and white. Among the more astute observers were Gunnar Myrdal, who chronicled "the American dilemma"—the distinction between rhetoric and reality in matters related to race—and W. E. B. DuBois, who predicted that the major social problem of the twentieth century would be the problem of color.

A distinction must be made between a general cultural piety about social equality and specific social policies directed toward educational concerns. The two are not necessarily complementary; in the United States they are frequently in conflict.

Social policy and social behavior in the United States created inequities which generally resulted in whites having advantages and opportunities that people of color did not have. Racial prejudices, hostilities, and even violence have prevented African-Americans and Hispanics from contributing fully to the development of the society. Even until the middle of the twentieth century, legal segregation was required in parts of the United States, highlighting the belief that whites were superior to people of other races (see Weinberg 1977). Where there was no legal requirement, custom—including residential patterns—achieved, and still achieves, the same result (Calmore 1986, Hodgkinson 1985).

In 1966 the National Advisory Commission on Civil Disorders warned that the United States was "moving toward two societies, one black and one white, separate and unequal." The country now faces "the possibility of fractionalizing into three societies: one Black, one white, and one Hispanic, still separate and still unequal" (Harvey 1985a, p. 48).

While practice has changed slowly, some progress has been made in reducing racially discriminatory policies in the United States, and much of this progress has been fairly recent.

Following the civil rights movement of the 1960s, which raised social consciousness and concern about the inherent unfairness of the society to nonwhite people, the development of affirmative action was considered a policy that would lead to significantly greater involvement of ethnic minorities in the American social and economic mainstream.

Measures taken to amend past social injustices often draw criticism. For example, actions to redress Japanese-Americans imprisoned during World War II and to compensate Native Americans for lands stolen from them have been denounced by some individuals and groups. These cases illustrate fellow citizens that have been treated unfairly by the majority simply because of their ethnicity.

Affirmative action brings to the surface some of the paradoxical aspects of our national experience. It deals with individual upward mobility as well as structural and institutional resistance. It contrasts initiating social change with maintaining the status quo. It challenges perceptions of quality along with interpretations of inequality. And it reflects a social rhetoric that speaks of inclusion and a social reality that practices exclusion (Harvey 1987).

Why Is It Important to Have a Diverse Faculty?

The initiation of affirmative action was partly based on the realization that colleges and universities occupy a unique position in society because of the opportunities they provide their members to challenge their individual and social perspectives and values. Further, colleges serve a select group of young people who acknowledge that part of the institutions' function is to challenge their pre-existing ideas. Therefore, faculty hirings at colleges and universities can influence the nation's readiness to benefit from the multicultural nature of our society in many ways: by providing both minorities and nonminorities with role models; by preparing minority youth to assume leadership roles; and by supporting minority-related scholarship.

The potential for university settings to meet these goals is undermined by the continuing absence of minorities in higher education. For Hispanics, faculty representation in the predominantly white institutions has increased only marginally since the introduction of affirmative action, to a rate of 1.8 percent in 1983 (*Chronicle of Higher Education* 1986, p. 24). African-Americans actually held a smaller share of faculty positions in 1985 than in 1977 (Green 1989, p. 82), and represented about 2.2 percent of the faculty at predominantly white colleges and universities in 1984 (Sudarkasa 1987, p. 4; see also Andrulis 1975; Blackwell 1983; Exum 1983; Harvey and Scott-Jones 1985).

African-American and Hispanic faculty members bring to the campus new perspectives based on their experiences and backgrounds. Their presence effectively serves to discredit the idea that scholarship and academic excellence are the sole province of white faculty. They provide role models for minority students and tangible examples of their capabilities to majority students, many of whom have not encountered a person of color in a position of authority (Blackwell 1981, 1983, 1987). White students, faculty, and administrators often assume that a competent African-American or Hispanic professor or administrator is an "exceptional overachiever," but this assumption is challenged when there are relatively many African-American and Hispanic faculty in an institution and when they are distributed across several academic areas (Harvey and Scott-Jones 1985).

The continued prevalence of residential racial separation in the United States has caused most white youngsters to have only intermittent contact with their African-American or Hispanic peers as they progress through childhood and adolescence. Further, too few white children encounter African-Americans or Hispanics in positions of power or authority, though they are quite likely to see them in deferential or subservient positions. These situations, along with the historical and contemporary stereotyping of nonwhite people, contribute to the development of negative perceptions among white students—perceptions that they are apt to take along with them to their chosen college or university (Harvey 1981).

It is critical for college students, before they move into positions of leadership and influence, to encounter and interact with instructors who are members of various racial and ethnic groups in order to quell effectively the myth about the intellectual and cultural inferiority of minority groups (Massey 1987). Otherwise, society runs the risk of carrying forward these long-standing myths into yet another generation (Harvey 1986).

Higher Education before Affirmative Action
The statistics on the presence of African-American and His-

panic faculty illustrate the important role that colleges and universities have played in maintaining racial segregation in the United States. Broadly speaking, these citadels of knowledge and learning, with occasional exceptions, have opted to go along with—rather than challenge—the prevailing attitudes and practices that have historically relegated African-Americans and Hispanics to second-class citizenship. Higher education institutions in the South did not challenge the appropriateness of the *de jure* segregation. Rather, they resisted desegregating their facilities even after these laws were ruled unconstitutional. Even in the North, where segregation was not legally required, African-Americans were discouraged from enrolling in local colleges and universities until the middle of the twentieth century (see Weinberg 1977).

Some scholars at these institutions have, throughout the history of the United States, developed theoretical models and intellectual rationales for the academic, social, and moral superiority of European thought, then used these arguments to justify the continued exploitation of nonwhite people and their exclusion from the mainstream of the society (see Weinberg 1977). Beginning with the depiction of Native Americans as ignorant savages, and continuing with the characterization of African slaves as subhumans, some academicians have endorsed the concepts of white supremacy and Western European cultural hegemony as fundamental truths (Marable 1983). Even in contemporary times, the patently unscientific concepts of genetic determination espoused by Arthur Jensen (1969)—and the current debates on the value of exploring non-Western ideas in the undergraduate core curriculum—are examples of this Eurocentric bias (see Bloom 1987, Hirsch 1987).

Any discussion of affirmative action must recall the historical factors leading to this solution. Before World War II, "Hispanics were nearly invisible in academia" (Wilson 1987, p. 11). By 1900, Mexican-Americans were permitted to attend the few existing "Mexican" schools. Except for a small group of wealthy Mexican-Americans, educational opportunities did not exist (Weinberg 1977, p. 286).

Before 1945, Hispanics were essentially enrolled in a few Catholic colleges (*Educational Record* 1988, p. 17). In 1900 the University of Puerto Rico was established as a normal school; it began to offer college instruction 10 years later

(*Educational Record* 1988, p. 17).

A national survey of college faculty in 1972-73 reported that there were slightly over 1,500 faculty who identified themselves as Mexican American or Chicano, and about 600 were in community colleges (Bayer 1972a, 1972b).

African-Americans were excluded from participating in higher education from the 1600s to the mid-1800s. By 1865, fewer than 30 African-Americans had graduated from a college or university in the United States, which marked the end of the Civil War and the subsequent emancipation of African-American slaves (Weinberg 1977, p. 6). Major institutions, such as Princeton University and Brown University, refused to accept African-American students; Harvard Medical School accepted three African-Americans in 1850, but expelled them after a year at the insistence of white students and the concurrence of white faculty (Weinberg 1977, p. 6).

Antioch College and Oberlin College are notable exceptions to these exclusionary practices. Both colleges accepted African-American students, and about 4 to 5 percent of Oberlin's enrollment during the 1840s and 1850s was African-American (Weinberg 1977, p. 6). Even after the Civil War, southern state governments refused to contribute public funds for African-American higher education. Between 1876 and 1900, only about 13 African-Americans a year graduated from northern colleges and universities, one-third from Oberlin alone (Weinberg 1977, p. 7).

Members of academe must remember that, until recently, the color bar has been rigidly applied to membership in the faculty ranks of predominantly white colleges and universities, with a handful of exceptions for clearly distinguished scholars. William Exum (1983) reports that in the 1850s, Charles L. Reason was a professor in a school founded by abolitionists— New York Central College. The African-American Jesuit priest, Father Patrick Healey, climbed the ranks from instructor to president of Georgetown University in 1873. The acclaimed historian W. E. B. DuBois was assistant instructor at the University of Pennsylvania from 1896 to 1897, but was never offered a permanent post there or at any other predominantly white institution. William A. Hinton began service at Harvard in 1918 where he held the rank of instructor for 26 years and that of lecturer for 3 years before finally being appointed professor in 1949, one year before he retired (Exum 1983, p. 385).

Lack of qualified applicants was not the reason for maintaining all-white faculties. In 1936, a sizable group of African-Americans with Ph.D.s was available for employment, but fully 80 percent of them taught in three African-American institutions: Atlanta, Fisk, and Howard Universities (Weinberg 1977, p. 9). "Blacks were thus subjected to a rigid negative employment quota of 100 to 0, which enforced an affirmative action program on behalf of segregation" (Weinberg 1977, p. 9).

In 1941, the Julius Rosenwald Fund, through a survey, was able to identify two tenured full-time African-American faculty in predominantly white institutions (*Educational Record* 1988, p. 19). Since many of the institutions that responded to the survey indicated that they could not locate African-American faculty, the Rosenwald Fund distributed the names of 200 African-Americans with Ph.D.s representing 26 different disciplines, and 300 African-Americans with M.A.s (*Educational Record* 1988, p. 19). Not one of these was hired.

Other efforts by the Rosenwald Fund also failed, but finally in 1945 when the Fund offered to pay their salaries, the University of Chicago hired Allison Davis in the sociology department, and Olivet College in Michigan hired Cornelius Golightly in the department of philosophy (*Educational Record* 1988, p. 19). Seven years later however, the University of Chicago refused to hire the eminent African-American sociologist E. Franklin Frazier because the wives of white professors would object (Weinberg 1977, p. 11).

Perhaps the only African-American professors and administrators at predominantly white institutions during this era were Walter F. Anderson, who in 1946 was chair of the music department at Antioch College, and Madeline Clarke Foreman, who in 1947 was chair of the biology department at William Penn College in Oscaloosa, Iowa (*Ebony* 1947, p. 16).

When the Rosenwald Fund sent letters to more than 500 college presidents in 30 northern states, 400 never replied. Those who did typically replied, "It isn't that we discriminate against the Negro race as such, it's just that our entire college is white" (*Ebony* 1947, p. 16). Others suggested that a segregated college was best for African-American students and teachers.

So few African-Americans held faculty positions at predominantly white institutions in the early twentieth century that the ones who were in such posts could be named and described individually. In 1947, *Ebony Magazine* estimated that out of 3,000 African-Americans who listed their occupation as "college teacher," only 78 had ever taught in predominantly white schools. These 78 held jobs at one of 43 northern colleges, either as full-time professors or temporary lecturers. More than one-third of all African-American instructors at predominantly white colleges were in New York City (*Ebony* 1947, p. 16).

Exum (1983, p. 385) further reports that by 1950, only 72 of the 1,051 white colleges and universities surveyed employed African-American professors; most of those were visiting instructors for one term or one year. By 1958 there were only 200 full-time African-American faculty members at predominantly white colleges and universities, and by 1961 that number had increased to 300. In 1960 African-Americans comprised 3 percent of all faculty in the United States and were heavily concentrated in historically African-American schools. By 1968-69 the percentage fell to 2.2 percent of the total. By 1972-73, African-Americans comprised 2.9 percent of all college and university faculty. By 1976, African-Americans were 4.4 percent of all faculty and heavily concentrated in historically African-American institutions. In 1979, African-Americans were still 4.4 percent of the full-time faculty in the nation. Not until the late 1960s did colleges in the United States begin to feel even slight pressure from the federal government to employ nonwhite faculty, and the results were exceedingly minimal (Weinberg 1977).

The G.I. Bill grants following World War II provided the initial impetus to diversify the student body. This generation of educated minorities provided the bulk of the minority faculty and administrators recruited into predominantly white institutions during the substantial opening of opportunity between 1964 and 1974 (Wilson 1987, p. 11).

Presumably, colleges and universities should not have needed governmental prodding to hire African-Americans and Hispanics for their faculties. In settings where intellect is nominally the most valued quality, the prejudices and irrationalities of the less educated would scarcely be expected to exist. After all, institutions of higher education would ostensibly be more interested in the quality of a person's mind than the color of the person's skin. This presumption is not supported by the record, however, which clearly shows that prior to the initiation of affirmative action, there were practically no African-American or Hispanic faculty members in predominantly white colleges and universities (Wilson 1987). Even though members of these two underrepresented groups had obtained doctoral degrees, frequently from the same institutions as their white counterparts, faculty positions were not available to them (Menges and Exum 1983, Reed 1983).

Although some moments in U.S. history are unpleasant to recall, it is important to remember that only a generation ago it was unlawful for African-Americans and whites in some places in the United States to attend the same college, let alone teach at the same institution. By law and by custom, discrimination against African-American and Hispanic people has been systemic and pervasive (Weinberg 1977).

As the mechanism through which larger numbers of African-Americans and Hispanics were expected to gain access to the faculty ranks of predominantly white institutions, affirmative action has been the twentieth century equivalent of "40 acres and a mule"—a phrase referring to compensation that was proposed, but not paid, for newly-freed African-American slaves for the discrimination and injustice that they had experienced. Before affirmative action, colleges and universities were both actively and passively supporting, if not advocating, racial segregation on their campuses and in the larger society.

Defining Affirmative Action
Though the term affirmative action is frequently used, its range of definitions leads to widespread misinterpretation and misunderstanding. Affirmative action has been called

> *government-fostered and voluntary action by public and private organizations going beyond the cessation of formal discriminatory practices . . . organizations must act positively, affirmatively, and aggressively to remove all barriers, however informal or subtle, that prevent access by minorities and women to their rightful places in the employment and educational institutions of the United States* (Benokraitis and Feagin 1978, p. 1).

Affirmative action has also been referred to as
> *a series of positive steps designed to eradicate the vestiges of past and current discrimination by ensuring that individuals not traditionally associated with various educational, social, and political institutions, and not found in*

adequate numbers in various professional and non-professional positions of employment, are actively sought, encouraged, and given opportunities to become affiliated with those institutions at every level of employment and human involvement (Reed 1983, p. 333).

Another perspective is that affirmative action is
a series of presidential executive orders, rules, and procedures, designed to protect minorities, such as Blacks, Puerto Ricans, Mexican-Americans, and American Indians from discrimination in employment, housing and education (Simmons 1982, p. vii).

From these definitions, one can conclude that affirmative action is a response to a history of discriminatory attitudes and actions against nonwhite people that prevented them from realizing opportunities that were available to whites, even when the nonwhites had equal or superior qualifications.

Affirmative action policies began on June 25, 1941 when President Franklin D. Roosevelt issued Executive Order 8802 requiring nondiscrimination in employment in all industries receiving defense contracts (Wilson 1985). The term "affirmative action" was first used in 1961 in Executive Order 10925, issued by President John F. Kennedy, which established the President's Committee on Equal Employment Opportunity (Wilson 1985).

President Lyndon Johnson frequently receives credit for initiating affirmative action because he signed Executive Order 11246 in September 1965 and amended it in 1972 to apply to educational institutions. The original order contained two major requirements: Nondiscrimination from all federal contractors, and affirmative action on the part of contractors to overcome the effects of past discrimination (Ohio State University 1985). Determining underutilization and planning means to overcome underutilization was the major effort (Henry 1985).

Kennedy's order was of more symbolic importance, but Johnson's order was more far-reaching, since he established the Office of Federal Contract Compliance Programs (OFCCP), required the development of written affirmative action plans, and established official penalties for noncompliance (see Wilson 1985). President Johnson signed Executive Order 11375 in 1967 which added "sex" to the categories prohibited

Affirmative action is a response to a history of discriminatory attitudes and actions against nonwhite people that prevented them from realizing opportunities that were available to whites.

from discrimination (Wilson 1985).

Johnson had envisioned the development of a "Great Society" that would include African-Americans and Hispanics as full participants, and this was an important step toward realizing that goal (Carter 1981). The significance of establishing OFCCP was that it marked the first serious implementation of an antidiscrimination policy that went beyond passive nondiscrimination. OFCCP required any entity with 50 or more employees, or receiving $50,000 or more in federal contracts, to file an affirmative action plan (Wilson 1985).

"Affirmative action" was not defined until 1970 when President Richard Nixon issued Order No. 4, which stated:

> *An affirmative action program is a set of specific and results-oriented procedures to which a contractor commits itself to apply every good faith effort. The objective of those procedures plus such efforts is equal employment opportunity* (Wilson 1985, pp. 18–19).

Affirmative action established as a matter of public policy the federal government's intention to use its powers on behalf of the victims of racial discrimination, so that they could gain access to positions and opportunities previously unavailable to them. Effective affirmative action requires equal consideration for all applicants for faculty positions, as well as for tenure and promotions. Enforcement activity can be initiated in three ways: (1) by a complaint by an individual or group, (2) through required compliance reviews specified in the contract, and (3) through periodic compliance reviews (Ohio State University 1985, p. 30).

The move from the compliance approach in affirmative action to a cultural pluralism approach is cited in *Making Affirmative Action Work in Higher Education* (Carnegie Council on Policy Studies in Higher Education 1975). The council stated that affirmative action should focus more on fair processes than on statistical projections. Similarly, in *Affirmative Action in the 1980s*, the U.S. Commission on Civil Rights (1981) clearly identified affirmative action as a remedy for past and continuing discrimination (see Henry 1985).

Enforcement of any policy, however, is facilitated by the degree of its acceptance. Public debate on the merits of affirmative action continues, and questions continue to be raised on just who should be required to overcome the effects of past discrimination.

Opponents of affirmative action object to this approach to achieving a greater measure of social equity for several reasons, even though they may be willing to support other movements that oppose discrimination. They point out some examples of what affirmative action opponents find irksome:

- Affirmative action laws have been more specific and action-oriented than other antidiscrimination measures.
- The official measures focusing on affirmative action have been broader in their scope than previous governmental action.
- Affirmative action places strong emphasis on active non-discrimination and on results.
- There are a range of sanctions for noncompliance with affirmative action requirements (Benokraitis and Feagan 1978).

Insofar as phrases can be used to depict a particular social climate or attitude, affirmative action can be thought of as a corollary to another term, "benign neglect," which suggests that the government ignore the problems faced by African-American and Hispanic Americans, presuming that they would somehow disappear. The difference lies in the concept of activism or energetic involvement as contrasted with passivity or inaction. At least in theory, affirmative action implies that the affected institutions or corporations should translate general principles into specific actions and attempt to remedy the effects of prior discrimination by actively seeking out and offering opportunities to the victims.

The failure of affirmative action programs rests with a fundamental question of who "owns" the problem: The institution or the structure that creates and perpetuates inequality, or the affected individual or group? Government policy recognizes that it is the colleges, not minorities, that are the targets of affirmative action programs. Thus, programs in institutions of higher education must be designed to discover the factors that contribute to inequality. These programs must be established within an organizational framework sufficient to generate appropriate solutions. Otherwise, universities fail to embrace the resources, talents, and capabilities of the full range of our national human resources.

The Impact of Affirmative Action on Higher Education

Affirmative action was initiated in higher education in 1972 following the passage of the Equal Employment Opportunity Act. The responses to its introduction varied from enthusiastic acceptance to vehement rejection. Colleges and universities, or more precisely, the officials who were charged with the responsibilities of policy formation and implementation, had little choice but to follow guidelines on recruiting and hiring procedures issued by the government. The alternative was a possible fine, and ultimately, even the loss of federal financial support (Institute for the Study of Educational Policy 1978).

The monitoring, reporting, and advertising requirements of affirmative action, which might be regarded as intrusive in any institutional arena, can be of special concern to faculty members because they directly affect the collegial traditions through which faculty have been hired. One of the peculiar aspects of higher education is that, unlike most other areas of employment, new members of the professoriat gain admission by securing the approval and consent of senior colleagues, not necessarily administrative leaders of the institution.

By means of an institutional process known as the search committee, faculty members are able to approve or disapprove of aspirants who wish to join the ranks (Harvey 1988a, 1988b; Harvey and Scott-Jones 1985). This traditional hiring process did not entail specific guidelines for posting announcements, advertising, interviewing, or extending offers. Personal connections, associations, and friendships constitute what is called the "old-boy system," which was the mechanism through which vacant faculty positions were likely to be filled.

In addition, the relatively absolute power of the faculty to hire new members of the professoriat was somewhat altered by the involvement of the campus administration, at least to requiring that the various departments and units in the institution follow affirmative action guidelines in their search and hiring processes (Harvey 1988a). An overlay of procedures was devised, including completing various availability forms and advertising in a wider range of outlets than those that had been traditionally used, as a means of providing African-American and Hispanic candidates a greater chance to be named as faculty members.

Affirmative action and its implementation procedures are described in Executive Order 11246 (1965). According to the provisions of this act, institutions must project the number of African-Americans and Hispanics to be hired over a specific period of time and set numerical goals rather than quotas to gauge progress. The bill required steps to ensure that searches, hiring, and promotions are conducted in a non-discriminatory manner. Institutions must ensure that African-Americans and Hispanics are adequately notified of vacancies, have a fair chance to apply, receive careful consideration during the search, and have a fair opportunity for promotion if hired. These efforts were mandated, not because African-Americans and Hispanics lacked the credentials to be hired through past procedures, but because discrimination had been an integral part of previous hiring procedures (Fleming, Gill, and Swinton 1978).

But in the final analysis, many institutions have never really fundamentally modified their traditional methods for selecting new members, which means that the process remains in the hands of the existing faculty and is not a true partnership with the administration. The intended compliance with affirmative action that was announced by the administration could easily be thwarted by the faculty. Basically, faculty continue to choose faculty appointments, while administrators review and endorse those choices. Colleges and universities have thus been able to portray themselves as affirmative action institutions, but show minimal increases, zero increases, or even declines in the numbers of African-American and His-panic faculty that they employ, since "good faith" efforts, rather than concrete results, have been considered as satis-factory evidence of their intentions (Benokraitis and Feagin 1978, Exum 1983, Harvey 1988a).

Affirmative action in colleges and universities deserves spe-cial scrutiny on the actual results in its specific function to bring about diversity in faculty representation. In 1972-73, African-Americans held 2.9 percent of the total faculty posi-tions in higher education, including those who were on the faculties of the historically African-American institutions. Other minority groups (including Hispanics, but not Asians) held 2.8 percent of the total faculty positions (Reed 1983, p. 334).

These results reflect considerable resistance to affirmative action that has been manifested in some quarters of the pre-dominantly white institutions of higher education. Often, by accident or design, issues have come into play that slow down affirmative action efforts or negate them altogether, such as the following:

- Different perceptions of the availability of African-American and Hispanic candidates.
- Imprecise determination of how hiring goals are set, as well as minimum or maximum figures.
- Undefined or unclear departmental roles in meeting institutional goals.
- Disagreement on appropriate advertising outlets and recruitment procedures.
- Different criteria for evaluating nonwhite candidates.
- The conscientiousness of the institution in meeting its goals.
- The degree of positive leadership from chief academic officers.
- Sufficient funding for affirmative action staff (Menges and Exum 1983).

The pace at which colleges and universities have implemented affirmative action may surprise some observers who think of colleges and universities as bastions of liberal thought and left-wing political and social tendencies. While it may be true that causes that promote social justice and human rights often receive support on college campuses before they receive it from other segments of society, even professors who tend to be liberal about issues outside higher education can be quite conservative regarding proposed modifications within their own bailiwick (Harvey and Scott-Jones 1985). Affirmative action foments change. It is this modification of the existing process—the threat of withheld funds if the process is not followed, and perhaps a degree of discomfort with the possible outcomes if the policies are successfully applied—that engenders such forceful opposition.

As illustrated in this section, racism has been practiced in institutions of higher education just as it has in other segments of society. Since the higher education apparatus functioned effectively for those who held faculty positions, they saw no need for changing the standard operating methods. White males have been overwhelmingly predominant among the faculty; it is not unreasonable to suppose that many of them regarded affirmative action as an intrusion into a set of activities that they held to be their purview.

In the past, race was clearly an explicit factor for eliminating candidates for positions on the faculties of predominantly white colleges and universities. More subtle measures may currently be used to maintain the racial composition of these bodies as overwhelmingly white (Sudarkasa 1987). Affirmative action officially eliminates the possibility for faculty members openly and legally to discriminate on the basis of race when selecting a candidate to fill a vacant position. However, a review of the representation of African-Americans and Hispanics in faculty positions indicates that little change has occurred since affirmative action came into being (Coughlin 1986; Hill 1983; Menges and Exum 1983; Wilson and Melendez 1984, 1985, 1986).

THE SUPPLY OF AND DEMAND FOR
AFRICAN-AMERICAN AND HISPANIC FACULTY

Although virtually all institutions pay lip service to affirmative action—and examples of successful affirmative action programs do exist—African-Americans and Hispanics remain severely underrepresented on predominantly white college and university faculties. Yet, because affirmative action policies have received attention in higher education in the past, African-Americans and Hispanics are often assumed to have made significant gains in their struggle for access to faculty and administrative roles in colleges and universities. An examination of the current status of these scholars, however, reveals that the notion of substantial progress is, at best, wishful thinking. Harvey and Scott-Jones argue that "by no reasonable, commonly understood interpretation of available data can it be said that African-Americans (or Hispanics, as groups) are succeeding as faculty members in predominantly white institutions of higher education" (1985, p. 68; Sudarkasa 1987).

Fully two-thirds of the African-American faculty are at the African-American colleges and universities.

Issues of supply and demand further cloud the reality of the current status and future expectations for the inclusion of nonwhite faculty and administrators. Even when the number of Ph.D.s awarded to African-Americans increased (Reed 1983), "many searches for new faculty still concluded with a thoroughly remorseful committee chair explaining that the position is not being offered to an African-American or Hispanic scholar because 'we couldn't find any' " (Harvey and Scott-Jones 1985, p. 68).

The purposes of this section are to examine some statistics on both the current status of African-American and Hispanic scholars in predominantly white colleges and universities, to examine the issue of supply and demand for minority faculty, and to review some policy considerations and program practices which may affect the goal of increasing the numbers of African-American and Hispanic professors.

However, it must be noted that complete and systematic data are not available on minority faculty in the United States. William Exum points out that

Until the 1970s, public, and in some states, private colleges and universities, as well as projects funded by the federal government, were all prohibited by statute, government regulation, or the individual institution's choice, from collecting these data (National Research Council 1978)....What may have begun as an attempt to fight discrimination in

*higher education by prohibiting the identification of appli-
cants, students, or faculty by race, has instead helped perpetuate racial inequality by hindering attempts to monitor
progress* (1983, p. 384).

Since 1975, however, colleges and universities have been
required to compile and report survey data under Title VII
of the Civil Rights Act as amended by the Equal Employment
Opportunity Act of 1972 (Reed 1983, p. 334).

Educational statistics are available in vast quantities from
a variety of sources, including the Higher Education Research
Institute, the National Center for Education Statistics (NCES),
and the Office of Civil Rights (OCR) of the U.S. Department
of Education. Yet, all of the education statistics that one would
require are not available in usable form. For example, OCR
has not budgeted publication of its data in almost eight years,
and NCES does not provide published information on all of
its surveys (Wilson and Melendez 1984).

Status of African-American and Hispanic Faculty in Higher Education

The goal of affirmative action is the fair representation of ethnic groups at all levels of academe; that is, the proportion
of African-Americans and Hispanics in faculty positions should
equal their proportion in the national population (Fleming,
Gill, and Swinton 1978). According to the 1980 census, equi-
table representation on college and university faculties, for
example, would be approximately 11.7 percent for African-
Americans (Harvey and Scott-Jones 1985, p. 68) and 7.2 percent for Hispanics (American Council on Education 1987,
p. 6). Note that this definition of equity is based on the proportion of the total African-American population, not on the
proportion of African-American college graduates.

The reality, however, falls far short of the goal of equity
using either population-based or graduation-based criteria
(see Table 1). Wilson (1987, p. 12) reports that the number
of African-American faculty increased until 1976, then began
to decline. Hispanic faculty presence increased slightly during
the same period.

Different data sources tell a similar story:
- African-American faculty in 1981 comprised 4.2 percent
  of the total higher education faculty, down from 4.4 percent in 1979 (Sudarkasa 1987, p. 4; Exum 1983, p. 385;

TABLE 1

**FULL-TIME FACULTY IN HIGHER EDUCATION
BY RACE/ETHNICITY AND SEX
1975, 1983, AND 1985**

Race/ Ethnicity & Sex	1975 Number	Percent	1983 Number	Percent	1985 Number	Percent	Percentage Change 1975-1985
White	409,947	91.7	440,505	90.7	439,767	90.0	7.3
Male	312,293	69.9	326,171	67.1	320,969	65.7	2.8
Female	97,654	21.9	114,334	23.5	118,798	24.3	21.7
African-American	19,746	4.4	19,571	4.0	20,283	4.1	2.7
Male	10,894	2.4	10,541	2.2	11,053	2.3	1.5
Female	8,852	2.0	9,030	1.9	9,230	1.9	4.3
Hispanic	6,323	1.4	7,456	1.5	8,087	1.7	27.9
Male	4,573	1.0	5,240	1.1	5,683	1.2	24.3
Female	1,750	0.4	2,216	0.5	2,404	0.5	37.4

Notes: Figures include African-American faculty at historically African-American institutions. Figures may not add up to 100 percent since figures for Asians and Native Americans are not shown here.

Source: American Council on Education 1988, p. 32. Reprinted by permission

Wilson 1985).
- African-American administrators comprised 6.8 percent of all administrators in 1981, down from 7.4 percent in 1979 (Sudarkasa 1987, p. 4).
- figures available from the U.S. Equal Employment Opportunity Commission show that, between 1977 and 1984, the percentage of full-time African-American faculty at four-year state institutions dropped to 4 percent from 4.3 percent (*Black Issues in Higher Education* 1987, p. 5).

These statistics conceal a situation that is even less encouraging to affirmative action advocates than the small numbers convey, because most of the African-American faculty and administrators are employed at traditionally African-American institutions. In the 1970s, between two-thirds and three-quarters of African-American faculty were in predominantly African-American colleges and universities (Exum 1983, p. 385; Fleming et al. 1978). Over half of the African-American administrators employed in higher education are in the African-American institutions, which are located in 19 states and the District of Columbia. Fully two-thirds of the African-

American faculty are at the predominantly African-American colleges and universities in those states (National Center for Education Statistics 1985).

In contrast, whites constitute nearly 39 percent of the faculty and 16 percent of the administrators at the traditionally African-American institutions. "Many higher education officials, and indeed, many desegregation researchers, consider the Black institutions to be 'too Black' while the white institutions are perceived as 'integrated'" (Wilson and Melendez 1985, p. 18; see also Burch 1988, p. 8).

Yet in 1984, African-American faculty employed by predominantly white colleges and universities constituted only about 2.2 percent of the total faculty. African-American administrators constituted only about 2.5 percent of the staff in these institutions. African-Americans make up only 2 percent, and Hispanics less than one percent, of faculties in the higher education mainstream, particularly in four-year and research institutions (Wilson 1987, p. 12).

Equally disappointing is that during the height of the period favoring the inclusion of minorities in the mainstream of higher education, the plurality of that inclusion was in the marginal and peripheral programs and positions most vulnerable to elimination (Wilson 1987). Many minority faculty were hired in African-American studies, Latino studies, and bilingual education often as adjunct faculty and lecturers rather than in professorial and tenure-track positions. Similarly, minority administrators were often appointed as directors of programs specifically established for minority and disadvantaged students, such as Upward Bound, TRIO, and affirmative action programs.

Supply and Demand Issues

Frequently, the stated reason for the tiny number of African-American and Hispanic faculty members in predominantly white colleges and universities is that qualified persons are in short supply. This contention is reminiscent, in a way, of the situation in the 1940s when the Rosenwald Fund made lists of qualified African-American academicians available to various institutions and these persons were not offered positions (see the previous section).

"We Can't Find Any"

One of the biggest prevailing myths of affirmative action in higher education is that faculty hiring is primarily a result of the availability of minorities with the appropriate terminal degree (Harvey and Scott-Jones 1985, Wilson 1987). "The assumption is that, with minorities holding doctorates being in short supply, those with the requisite degrees would be 'hot ticket' items and the larger problem would be in finding more" (Wilson 1987, p. 12).

Proponents of the availability pool rationale for the low numbers of African-American and Hispanic faculty can readily find data to support their argument. The available faculty pool is limited by four factors: The small or declining number of African-Americans and Hispanics with Ph.D.s; the under-representation of minorities in particular disciplines and fields such as science and engineering; the concentration of African-American and Hispanic doctorates in the fields of education, humanities, and social sciences; and the trend toward non-academic employment among Ph.D. holders. For example, only about 900 doctorates are awarded to African-Americans annually, a sharp decline since the 1970s (see Mingle 1987a; see also Table 2, next page).

African-Americans and Hispanics earn relatively few of the doctorates awarded to U.S. citizens in graduate science and engineering programs. For example, a National Science Foundation Survey of doctorates awarded from July 1986 to June 1987 found that while Hispanics have earned steadily higher numbers of science doctorates since 1978, the numbers remain low (160 in 1978 and 292 in 1987). On the other hand, while the number of African-Americans earning science doctorates increased between 1975 and 1978, the number has declined since then (278 or 2.1 percent in 1978; 222 or 1.8 percent in 1987). "Blacks are the only racial and ethnic group in which this is occurring," said Susan Hill (*Washington Post*, as cited in *Black Issues in Higher Education*, 1988, p. 19).

Without a doubt, there is serious underrepresentation of minorities in particular disciplines and fields. Hispanics have tended to be concentrated in education and the humanities. In 1977, 60 percent of all African-Americans with doctorates were in education and the social sciences. In 1980-81, 53 percent of all African-Americans with doctorates were in education and 20 percent were in the social sciences (Exum 1983, p. 385). By 1985, half of all doctorates earned by African-

TABLE 2

TOTAL DOCTORATE DEGREES BY
RACE/ETHNICITY FOR SELECTED YEARS

	1975-1976 Total	%	1980-1981 Total	%	1984-1985 Total	%	Percent Change 1975-1985
African-American	1,213	3.6(a)	1,265	3.9	1,154	3.6	-4.9
Men	771	3.0(b)	694	3.1	561	2.6	-27.2
Women	442	5.7(c)	571	5.6	593	5.4	+34.1
Hispanic	396	1.2	456	1.4	677	2.1	+71.1
Men	289	1.1	277	1.2	431	2.0	+49.1
Women	107	1.4	179	1.7	246	2.2	+130.0
Asian/ Pac. Islander	583	1.7	877	2.7	1,106	3.4	+89.7
Men	480	1.8	655	2.9	802	3.8	+67.1
Women	103	1.3	222	2.2	304	2.8	+195.1
White	27,434	81.2	25,908	78.9	23,934	74.1	-12.8
Men	20,852	80.2	17,310	76.6	15,017	41.9	-27.9
Women	6,582	84.6	8,598	83.9	8,917	81.0	+35.5

a. Degrees awarded to this group as a percentage of all doctorates awarded that year.
b. Degrees awarded to men in this group as a percentage of all doctorates awarded to men that year.
c. Degrees awarded to women in this group as a percentage of all doctorates awarded to women that year.

Source: American Council on Education, Sixth Annual Status Report (1987) on Minorities in Higher Education.

Americans were still in the field of education (see Table 3 on next page).

In 1985, African-Americans earned 503 doctorates in education, 205 in the social and behavioral sciences, and 75 in the humanities. African-Americans received 7 doctorates in mathematics, 3 in computer science, 23 in chemistry, 34 in engineering, 18 in life sciences and only 4 in physics. Not one African-American received a doctorate in such specializations as pharmaceutical chemistry, theoretical chemistry, biomedical engineering, operations research, embryology, statistics, and American studies. The absence of African-Americans who earn a doctorate in basic health sciences such as immunology, microbiology, anatomy, bacteriology, embryology, and related fields is a serious impediment to

TABLE 3. 1977-1986
AFRICAN-AMERICANS RECEIVING Ph.D.s

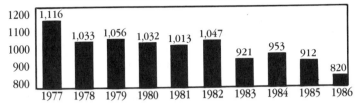

Types of Doctorates Earned in 1986 (PhDs Awarded African-American)

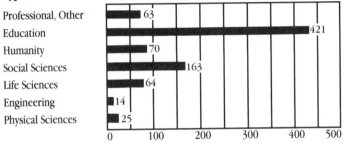

Source: National Research Council as reprinted in Black Issues in Higher Education, 1988, p. 8. Reprinted by permission

any effort to recruit and hire African-Americans for medical colleges and schools (see Cartwright 1987, Exum 1983, National Advisory Committee on Black Higher Education 1980a).

In addition to the uneven distribution by field, African-American Ph.D. recipients are older when they begin their graduate studies and take significantly longer to attain their degrees than whites, presumably for financial reasons (National Advisory Committee on Black Higher Education 1980a). African-American graduate students are more likely to be enrolled part-time and to be concentrated in master's degree programs (Exum 1983).

It is frequently argued that African-American and Hispanic students who complete baccalaureate programs are choosing nonacademic careers which offer higher salaries. For example, of the 137 African-American seniors in Harvard's class of 1980, only 2 chose to enter graduate work in the arts and sciences (Exum 1983, p. 388). In 1975, more than two-thirds of the African-American Ph.D. recipients planned to pursue an academic career, compared with less than half in 1986. The proportion of whites planning academic careers dropped from 60 to 48 percent during that same period (Brown 1988). However, the larger pool of white doctorate holders caused faculty shortages in only a few fields (Green 1989).

Despite the Availability Pool Issues, Supply Seems to Exceed Demand

The availability pool of African-Americans and Hispanics who hold doctorates is definitely a problem: There are too few of these individuals, and they are not evenly distributed across the range of academic fields. But, even when the availability pool was somewhat larger and faculty hiring was on the increase, African-American and Hispanic academicians did not receive faculty positions in predominantly white institutions in proportion to their representation in the total pool of Ph.D.s. Today, even in fields with relatively large pools of potential faculty members such as education and social work, few African-Americans or Hispanics have been hired. The lack of affirmative action progress for African-Americans and Hispanics cannot be explained fully by arguments about the availability pool. If the affirmative action goals of the past two decades had been conscientiously pursued, the percentage of African-Americans and Hispanics on college and university faculties would have increased during that period of time.

For example, fewer African-American scholars entered the professorial ranks in 1979 than in 1975. This decline occurred when the number of full-time faculty positions increased by more than 5,000 and the number of African-Americans receiving Ph.D.s increased by more than 200 (Boyd 1988, Harvey and Scott-Jones 1985, Reed 1983, Wilson 1987, Wilson and Melendez 1983).

The situation has been somewhat similar for Hispanic faculty. Their representation as a percentage remained essentially stable while the overall number of faculty positions was increasing and when affirmative action was official policy. Between 1975 and 1977, the total number of Hispanic faculty members grew from 6,323 to 6,842. In the next two years, however, the number grew by only 67, from 6,842 to 6,909— even though 439 Hispanics received doctorates in 1978-79 alone. Despite the growth in the total number of faculty positions held by Hispanics between 1975 and 1979, the proportionate increase in Hispanic representation only grew from 1.4 percent in 1975 to 1.5 percent in 1979 (Wilson and Melendez 1987).

The affirmative action status of women of color is similar to that of African-Americans and Hispanics overall. Despite overall progress for women, Hispanic, Asian, and Native American women did not advance much in administrative and faculty positions between 1979 and 1981, and the number of African-American women in these positions declined during this time (Rix 1987). A major prevailing myth in higher education is that minority women are "prime hires" because they represent two "protected groups." Reginald Wilson (1987) states that this notion is "unfortunately false." Those at the bottom of the professorial ladder in number, in rank, and in comparable salaries, are Hispanic and African-American women.

Another myth identified by Wilson (1987) is that minority Ph.D.s in science and engineering are so rare that they can command top salaries and that many colleges cannot afford them. Again, the data do not support this assertion. Science and engineering Ph.D. holders who received their degrees during the same period as their white colleagues, and who had similar work activities, attained tenure at 45.1 percent, significantly lower than the 61.3 percent for whites. They also attained promotions at a lower rate (Wilson 1987, p. 13; see also National Academy of Sciences 1987).

Those minorities who are hired as faculty members tend to be concentrated in the 114 predominantly African-American institutions; in the less prestigious colleges and universities; in public rather than private colleges; and in colleges which do not grant doctoral degrees (Exum 1983, p. 385; Fleming, Gill, and Swinton 1978). Minority faculty appear to be even more greatly underrepresented in two-year colleges—a situation that is noteworthy on two counts: Large proportions of minority students attend community colleges, and qualifications for faculty positions in the two-year college system do not normally require terminal degrees.

To summarize issues related to the supply and demand of African-American and Hispanic faculty, Exum (1983) points out that demand is usually related to both scarcity and desirability. While African-Americans and Hispanics are indeed scarce, questions remain about how highly they are valued by predominantly white colleges and universities.

It is important to stress and repeat the necessity of considerably increasing the number of minorities with doctorates.

Those at the bottom of the professorial ladder in number, in rank, and in comparable salaries, are Hispanic and African-American women.

But it is equally important to stress that we are not max-imally using those who are qualified and available (Wilson 1987, p. 12, emphasis in original).

With the decline of African-American participation in white institutions *following* affirmative action laws, it is apparent that most African-Americans have enrolled or been hired with-out any special or preferential treatment. The usual laws of supply and demand have not applied to African-Americans and Hispanics in higher education.

Quality of Faculty Life

Though statistics depict the seriousness of affirmative action failures numerically, they only hint at the gravity of the issue on qualitative aspects of the educational environment.

When there are a very small number of African-American or Hispanic faculty members in a given institution, the burdens of institutional and individual racism weigh heavily. The psychological safety associated with numbers is not avail-able to persons who work in these isolated situations. Demands on African-American and Hispanic faculty time and presence escalate. In the absence of a support group operating under the same circumstances, frustrations understandably mount (Sudarkasa 1987).

The quality of the work life for African-American and His-panic professors is characterized by differences in opportun-ities for sponsorship and mentors, perceptions about schol-arship dealing with ethnicity, and a variety of other work inequities.

Sponsorship and Mentors

One obstacle facing African-American and Hispanic faculty is the lack of effective sponsorship. The usual protective net-work of sympathetic senior faculty often does not exist. Research has shown that achievement for African-American graduate and professional school students is best predicted by the perception of opportunities to find a mentor (Hall and Allen 1982). The most successful academicians are those who attended the "best" graduate schools in their fields, had financial assistance, and were the proteges of well-established researchers (Cameron and Blackburn 1981, Merriam 1983). Yet African-American and Hispanic graduate students and junior faculty members are short on role models, mentors, and support networks.

Scholarship on Ethnicity

Many minority faculty also believe that their work is under-valued if they choose research topics related to ethnic groups (Valverde 1980). For example, Hispanic faculty are often "type cast" as specialists in ethnic matters rather than as "qualified" in a particular discipline. This perception has developed partly from the research interests of Hispanic faculty. The 1987 National Latino Faculty Survey found that two out of every three Hispanic faculty in the social sciences, education or the humanities wrote doctoral dissertations dealing with their own ethnic group, Latin American, minorities, or other related topics (Garza 1988).

Similarly, a 1986 affirmative action study found that a staggering percentage of Chicano faculty were heavily concentrated in Chicano Studies, and related departments and sub-specialties, such as Spanish. The study indicated that about 41 percent of the Hispanic faculty thought to be in the social sciences and humanities were actually employed by these ethnic studies programs (Garza 1988, p. 124).

Moreover, Hispanic participation in university committees is often related to ethnic factors. A survey of 149 Chicano faculty found that 43 percent of them are involved in affirmative action or ethnic community-related committees on campus; 57 percent were on committees dealing with the recruitment and retention of Chicano students (Garza 1988, p. 124). Similarly, 58 percent of the respondents in the 1987 National Latino Faculty Survey indicated that the administrative positions they have held were directorships, chairs and coordinators of programs concerned exclusively with equity issues such as affirmative action or language (Garza 1988).

Tenure

The American Council on Education's *Third Annual Status Report on Minorities in Higher Education* (Wilson and Melendez 1984) states that for all doctorates earned between 1960 and 1978, minority doctorate recipients are less likely to be hired on the tenure track or to obtain tenure in both the sciences and the humanities. The minority tenure rate exceeded whites only in the cohort of 1960-1969 degree recipients working in the sciences. In all other categories, minorities obtain relatively fewer tenured positions.

The report further illustrates that the incidence of tenure cannot be explained by different duties assigned to minority faculty: academically employed minorities held different types of positions with the same relative frequency as whites.

A recently published study by Shirley Vining Brown (1988) also reports that minority faculty are less likely to hold tenure than whites. Sixty-two percent of the African-American faculty in four-year colleges and 66 percent of the Hispanic faculty were tenured, compared with 71 percent of all faculty. However, Brown found that minority faculty were more likely than whites to be in tenure-track positions.

Work Inequities

In addition, African-American and Hispanic faculty commonly face problems of inequity. Studies report that they are subject to lower pay, heavier workloads, or other deterrents to advancement. They are clustered in lower ranks, part-time and nontenured positions, and special programs for minority students—inequities that stand even when the receipt date of the Ph.D. and entry into teaching are controlled (Exum 1983, p. 386). Many experience some form of harassment and frustration with inadequate grievance or appeals procedures.

These differences in the work life of minority and white faculty are not new. In October 1947, *Ebony* noted that "prestige rather than money is attracting most colored teachers into white colleges. One professor . . . is drawing a paltry $1,800 a year, less than Chicago street cleaners get" (*Ebony* 1947, p. 16). Ebony also noted that at Wayne University in Detroit, Charles Wesley Buggs carried the heaviest teaching load in the School of Medicine. He taught 546 hours, exceeding the maximum allowable teaching load of 400 hours (*Ebony* 1947, p. 18).

The African-American and Hispanic professoriat has often expressed its professional frustration, demoralization and lack of hope (*Black Issues in Higher Education* 1988, Burch 1988, Dennis and Silver 1988, Franklin 1988, O'Brien 1987). Hispanic and African-American faculty members are subjected to the aggravating aspects of the academic milieu without enjoying some of its compensating benefits: contemplation, independence, and social and intellectual stimulation from colleagues sharing the same interests and outlook (Benokraitis and Feagin 1978; Exum 1983; Scott 1981a, 1981b).

Once recruited, African-American and Hispanic faculty face distinctive and largely unacknowledged problems in pursuing their careers, which lead to difficulties in retention and promotion. Many of them suffer from unusual service and advising burdens; they are far more likely than their white male peers to be assigned high-workload/low-reward activities, such as large undergraduate classes and extensive committee work (Hornig 1979, Moore and Wagstaff 1974). Such workloads can diminish both research productivity and job satisfaction; often the problem goes unacknowledged because there is insufficient two-way communication between untenured faculty and their department chairs and college deans. (See Arciniega 1985, Menges and Exum 1983, and Valverde 1980. For a contrary view, see Elmore and Blackburn 1983.)

The stresses associated with the competing obligations of being role models and institutional servants are often unrecognized barriers to the achievement and mobility of African-American and Hispanic faculty (Black 1981, Escobedo 1980, Menges and Exum 1983, Valverde 1980). Ironically, these service burdens are often critical to the success of the minority presence on white campuses. Indeed, "colleges and universities need minority faculty . . . precisely because of the service roles they fill" in terms of being "buffers, mediators and interpreters" of minority concerns (Exum 1983, p. 395). Yet the individual careers of minority faculty can be damaged in the process of negotiating these dilemmas.

What Colleges Can Do
Department chairs and deans can begin to address these issues by recognizing that excessive committee work and student advising for African-American and Hispanic faculty is a fact of academic life—and will remain so until faculty representation mirrors student representation. It is totally unrealistic, for example, to advise African-American or Hispanic faculty to "just say no" to students from their groups seeking informal and undocumented advice or support in overcoming the same obstacles and frustrations they themselves had to face as students and professionals. These difficulties are compounded when these same faculty are asked to "represent" their ethnic groups, sometimes as mere window dressing, on a myriad of college or university committees. Instead, chairs and deans can regularly provide release time for research to compensate African-American and Hispanic faculty for excessive committee and advising workloads, and thus provide these faculty members with genuinely equal

opportunities to produce the research necessary for retention and promotion. Where appropriate, service activities in support of affirmative action goals should be rewarded in promotion and tenure considerations (Ohio State University 1985).

Chairs and deans also should assist in creating support and mentor networks for new faculty from targeted groups, who can often feel isolated and uninformed. Chairs and deans should routinely advise all untenured faculty of the actual, not ostensible, procedures and standards for tenure and promotion, and specifically inform them how to prepare dossiers appropriate to those standards and procedures (Ohio State University 1985).

As a matter of course, sincere commitment by a college or university to recruit African-American and Hispanic faculty also entails a commitment to fairness in supporting those faculty once they have been hired. The institutions must notice and respond to the special set of conditions in which African-American and Hispanic faculty find themselves, and not simply pretend that their situations are identical to that of their white counterparts. "Revolving door" retention records should be subject to the same budgetary and personnel sanctions as low-level recruitment efforts, and distinguished retention records should be rewarded through means that might include additional faculty slots (Ohio State University 1985).

Affirmative action activities aimed at promoting and retaining African-American and Hispanic faculty should devise ways of promoting faculty from targeted populations who disproportionately begin their careers in adjunct, part-time, or full-time temporary, nontenure track positions (Abel 1981); ensure truly professional review and recognition of excellence in nontraditional scholarship, e.g., African-American studies; ensure that salary equity exists and that multiple contributions of faculty from targeted populations to service, teaching, scholarship, mentoring, advising, and recruitment have been fully rewarded; conduct regular exit interviews and job satisfaction surveys containing affirmative action questions; and develop and publicize a strong policy against racial harassment (Ohio State University 1985).

Tomorrow's Professoriat: The Empty Pipeline

The current status of African-American and Hispanic faculty is not likely to be remedied solely through traditional means,

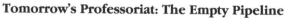

as shown by the statistics on minorities in the pipeline leading toward graduate and professional degrees and thereby enable them to compete for jobs in higher education. In 1969, 2,280 African-Americans with Ph.D.s were identified in a survey, less than 1 percent of the total (Ford Foundation 1969). Although Hispanics, especially Hispanic women, have made impressive gains in the number of doctorates earned since 1975, they continue to be one of the most underrepresented populations in higher education. African-Americans are the only minority group to actually experience declines in the number of degrees awarded at nearly all levels between 1975–76 and 1984–85; African-American men sustained the greatest loss (see Tables 1 and 2, Blackwell 1987, Sudarkasa 1987).

The pipeline issue can be examined by reviewing issues in secondary and undergraduate education, the graduate school admissions process, trends in graduate school enrollment, and doctoral degree candidates and recipients.

Secondary and Undergraduate Education

The "pipeline issue" suggests that one barrier to the increased participation of African-American and Hispanic scholars as faculty members is the lack of preparation provided to many minorities throughout the educational process. This issue has been substantiated by research which shows that minority students have faced, and continue to face, tremendous odds throughout their years of schooling (see Washington and LaPoint 1988, Weinberg 1977). Relatively few minority students have attended undergraduate educational institutions in the past, and even fewer went to graduate school (Preer 1981, Staples 1986).

Although the educational level of Americans has increased significantly over the past 20 years, African-Americans and Hispanics are far less likely than whites to enter and complete college. In 1985 23 percent of the white adults aged 25 to 29 had completed four or more years of college, compared to 11 percent for each of the two minority groups (Census Bureau 1987). Hispanics are at the greatest risk; the eligible pool of college-age Hispanic youth continues to decline because they do not complete high school (Mingle 1987). African-Americans, 13 percent of college-age youth, represent only 9.5 percent of all undergraduates and only 4.8 percent of all graduate students (Mingle 1987a).

Recent data indicate that the average SAT scores of all

minority students, except Hispanics, have risen since 1985. SAT scores for Mexican-American and Puerto Rican students fell in this period; the scores of whites also dropped slightly (*Chronicle of Higher Education* 1987, p. 1).

Graduate School Admissions Process

These declines in the numbers of African-American graduate students cannot be explained adequately by examining demographic factors or by reviewing trends in African-American undergraduate enrollment. Indeed, no similar declines for other minorities have occurred (Blake 1987). In fact, women and other minorities continued to increase their gains. No demographic reasons lie behind this decline. The absolute numbers of African-Americans aged 18 to 24 increased. The proportion of African-American high school graduates increased, as did their absolute numbers. Nevertheless, from a high point in or around 1979-1980, there has been a steady decline of African-American college attendance in almost all categories: enrollments of recent high school graduates, full-time attendees, and enrollment in four-year colleges. There may be questions about the accuracy of some of the data, but the trend for African-American college enrollment in the 1980s is down, no matter which data base is used (Arbeiter 1987).

One explanation for the failure of affirmative action to increase significantly the numbers of minority graduate students may lie with the graduate school admissions process. There are few African-American or Hispanic faculty to serve as role models and mentors in the recruitment process (Exum 1983). Eugene Cota-Robles, Vice-President for Academic Affairs at the University of California, argues that "admissions to graduate study are driven by faculty interests as opposed to institutional or societal interests" (*Chronicle of Higher Education* 1988, p. A17).

In this view, what is needed are programs which encourage faculty members to work with minority students, including increased state support for graduate fellowships. (The next section has a more detailed discussion of special recruitment programs and activities for graduate students).

Trends in Graduate School Enrollment

Both the absolute numbers and percentage of African-American school graduate enrollment are declining. In 1978,

the 61,923 African-American graduate students represented
6.2 percent of the total graduate enrollment; in 1980 both
the absolute number and percentage of African-American graduate enrollment had dropped to 60,138 and 5.5 percent,
respectively. The downward slide continued in 1982 when
the 54,907 African-American graduate students comprised
5 percent of the total graduate enrollment (see Table 4).

The full-time enrollment of African-Americans in professional schools also declined from 4.8 percent to 4.6 percent.
African-American enrollment in medical schools peaked at
6.3 percent in 1975; by 1985 it was down to 5.9 percent. The
percentage of master's degrees awarded to African-Americans
between 1976 and 1981 declined by 16 percent, a figure four
times greater than the decline for non-African-Americans.

While graduate school enrollment is declining for whites,
the decline for African-Americans is much sharper. Between
1976 and 1985, the number of African-American graduate students fell by 19 percent, compared to 5.4 percent for white
students between 1976 and 1984. The number of Hispanic
students rose by 20 percent but is still quite small in absolute
numbers. Proportionate to representation in the larger society,
Hispanics remain the least represented in higher education
(see Table 4; Carnegie Foundation for the Advancement of
Teaching 1987; Cartwright 1987).

TABLE 4
MINORITIES AND WOMEN
IN GRADUATE SCHOOL

	1976-1977	1984-1985	Change
African-Americans	65,352	52,834	-19.2
Hispanics	20,274	24,402	20.4
Asians	18,487	28,543	54.4
Women	467,155	503,525	7.8

Figures include U.S. citizens only.

SOURCE: Center for Statistics, U.S. Dept. of Education, as cited in *The Chron-icle of Higher Education,* September 10, 1986, p. 1.

Doctoral Degree Candidates and Recipients

Traditionally African-American colleges and universities clearly contribute to the supply of African-American faculty. About 55 percent of the 6,320 African-Americans who received doctorates between 1975 and 1980 received their undergraduate degrees from 87 traditionally African-American institutions. The other 45 percent received their baccalaureate degrees from 633 predominantly white institutions (see Higher Education Fact Sheet 1982; National Advisory Committee on Black Higher Education and Black Colleges and Universities 1980a, 1980b; Sudarkasa 1987, p. 6; Wilson and Melendez 1985).

Note that between 1975 and 1985 (see Table 2), the aggregate number and percentage of white males earning doctorates have diminished. The percentage of decrease is roughly equivalent to the percentage of decrease experienced by African-American males during that same time period. However, current faculty hiring patterns indicate that a decreased pool of white males may not lead to increased hiring of African-Americans and Hispanics. The overriding reality is that white males and females together hold approximately nine out of every 10 faculty positions in higher education including over one-third of the faculty positions at historically African-American institutions (Wilson and Melendez 1985, p. 18). Therefore, the loss in positions among white males can be accounted for mostly by gains made for white females.

Whites still seem to earn most doctorates. The National Research Council reported that in 1986, among doctorate recipients who were U.S. citizens, 91.1 percent were white, 3.6 percent were African-American, 2.5 percent were Hispanic, 2.3 percent were Asian and 0.4 percent were American Indian. Thus, all minorities earned about 8.6 percent of the doctorates in 1986, compared to 6.9 percent in 1976. In 1986, the number of African-Americans with doctorates decreased by 25 percent since 1976, while the number of Hispanics increased by 64 percent (see *Higher Education and National Affairs* 1988, p. 3). This rate of social change does not pose a threat to the status of whites in higher education.

In some instances, the decline in the pool of potential African-American faculty is occurring despite federal mandates and the presence of state funds for doctoral study. For example, Trent and Copeland (1987) found that the number of African-American doctoral students has declined in five southern states despite a federal mandate to increase the number of African-Americans with Ph.D.s. The states—Arkansas, Florida, Georgia, Oklahoma, and Virginia—awarded 78 doctorates to African-American students in 1983-84, six fewer than in 1975-1976, before the mandate took effect. Although those states had 24 percent of the nation's African-American undergraduates, they had only 7 percent of the African-American graduate students. These southern states were among 10 in a 1973 U.S. District Court ruling requiring the Department of Health, Education and Welfare's Office for Civil Rights to ensure that the public systems of higher education were desegregated and that the number of African-American graduate students enrolled increased. Yet the number of first-time graduate students enrolled fell to 757 in 1984, from a high of 1,218 in 1978. The study also reported that states with limited resources tended to focus on recruitment rather than on retention of African-American graduate students, resulting in "a revolving door" at the graduate level (Trent and Copeland 1987).

In some instances, the decline in the pool of potential African-American faculty is occurring despite federal mandates and the presence of state funds for doctoral study.

Barriers to Equal Access and Effective Affirmative Action

Wilson (1987) argues that despite the appearance of substantial change and diversity in the academy, this change had been to a great extent peripheral and more apparent than real. Moreover, the change that has occurred has been in the outer precincts of the higher education enterprise rather than within its heartland to any great degree. When decline occurs, it is most sharply evident in the most vulnerable part of higher education where most minorities reside.

The Carnegie Foundation concluded that it is important that a search for trends in participation at different levels of higher education by various groups not lose sight of equity concerns. With the notable exception of Asians, the proportion of minorities in higher education does not reach the level of their presence in the population. The disparity is likely to increase since population projections indicate that the numbers of minorities in the U.S. population will continue to grow.

Several barriers to equal access and effective affirmative action can be identified, including the lack of availability data, reduced federal support, philosophical debates, and inadequate financial aid.

Lack of Availability Data

It is argued that implementing affirmative action in universities is impeded because higher education does not have access to data appropriate for establishing utilization goals at colleges and universities. To establish these goals, administrators need availability data on the number of African-Americans and Hispanics available for faculty positions, but availability data for higher education is scarce and difficult to apply. However, it must be explicitly recognized that the availability of African-Americans and Hispanics is different from their recruitability (Higgerson and Hinchcliff-Pias 1982).

Recognition of the need for availability data must be quickly followed by the realization that the issue is more than one of just numbers or degrees, because a degree does not mean a job (Menges and Exum 1983). When qualified potential African-American and Hispanic faculty members are available, but still receive no positions in predominantly white colleges and universities, questions of fairness and equitability seem to be in order. When this situation occurs despite the presence of affirmative action policies, the effectiveness of these measures and the sincerity of the institutions that subscribe to them also seem to be open to question.

Reduced Federal Support

Many observers point to reduced support from federal-level decision-makers as a key role in the lack of affirmative action success. For example, following the presidential election in 1980, Senator Orrin Hatch of Utah announced that he would advocate a constitutional amendment to ban affirmative action programs that give preference to minorities and women in employment and education (Reed 1983, p. 345). Critics charge that the Reagan administration made a partly successful, broad-based attempt to reduce the government's gathering and use of information on the participation of African-Americans in education (*Black Issues in Higher Education* 1985, p. 2).

Many observers believe that the beginning of the Reagan presidency coincides with limited enforcement of civil rights laws such as affirmative action. During the Reagan era, the number of employees in the U.S. Department of Education's Office of Civil Rights declined from 1,025 in 1981 to 809 in 1987. Travel budgets for investigators in 10 regional offices declined from $1.7 million in 1981 to under $675,00 in 1987

(*Educational Record* 1988, p. 17).

Philosophical Debates

The momentum of affirmative action achieved from the 1960s until the mid-1970s has been halted. Blake (1987) argues that the mid-1970s to the mid-1980s are years of lost opportunities. In retrospect, Blake identifies two factors which undermined the momentum. First of all, the good news of the previous decade—1965 to 1975—was considered so good and so irreversible that the bad news was underestimated. Dramatic and fundamental changes had been made, and it was believed that attempts to include African-Americans and Hispanics in the higher education system were being made on a broad basis. The bad news was that a national debate flared over the application of affirmative action to faculty hiring and scarce places in professional schools. Affirmative action, preferential treatment, and reverse discrimination were arrayed on one side—merit, standards, and qualifications on the other. Those committed to the methods of the 1960s and early 1970s for getting fair treatment for African-Americans and Hispanics were forced to defend themselves against charges that they were the enemies of merit and historical standards of qualification. With the Alan Bakke case in 1979, affirmative action policies that were the basis for African-American and Hispanic progress were cast in doubt.

Inadequate Financial Aid

As a second factor, Blake cites the federal legislation in 1978 that put middle-income students under the tent of federal financial aid. To this day, this policy shift haunts the debate on how much money is enough to finance needy students.

Limits on the total aid availability have significantly increased unmet need and shifted more and more aid from grants to loans for even the lowest income students. This problem is accelerated by the shift from grants to loans. For many low income students, "a loan is tantamount to no money at all" (Tendaji Ganges, Upward Bound, quoted in *Newsweek on Campus,* February 1987, p. 16).

The importance of financial aid can also be illustrated by noting that the first significant wave of campus diversity occurred with the G.I. Bill grants opportunities following World War II (Wilson 1987, p. 11). Therefore, many academics and federal officials point to declining federal student aid grants as contributing to the decline in the number of African-American graduates (for example, see NSF's study of science doctorates earned by minorities) (*Black Issues in Higher Education* 1988, p. 19).

Ernst Benjamin, the general secretary of the AAUP, points to rising education costs as a major reason for these declines, along with the financial aid trend of awarding more loans than grants (Burch 1988, p. 8). Alan W. Ostar, President of the American Association of State Colleges and Universities, points to several barriers keeping minority students out of graduate schools, such as the new tax law that designates scholarship or work-study funds as not tuition taxable.

African-American students are two to five times more likely than white students to rely on various federal aid programs to finance their undergraduate education (Exum 1983, p. 386). Burdened with debt from their undergraduate education, minority graduate students are more likely to enroll part time, take longer to finish their graduate work, and enroll in masters rather than doctoral programs (Exum 1983).

Exum (1983) outlines the difficulties which African-American graduate students have faced in obtaining financial support for their education. African-Americans are more dependent than whites or foreign students on their own earnings, federal loans, and/or other commercial loans to pay for their graduate education. Of those African-Americans receiving doctorates in 1978, only 2 received a National Science Foundation traineeship out of 422 awarded that year, and African-Americans received 16 of the 725 fellowships awards (Exum 1983, p. 388). Moreover, the distribution of both federal and institutional financial support has tended to reflect and reinforce the uneven distribution of African-American doctorates by field (Exum 1983). For example, nearly half of the National Defense Education Act Fellowships awarded to African-American doctorate recipients in 1978 were in education, compared to 15.1 percent for whites (Exum 1983, p. 388).

The fact that African-American student enrollment doubled between 1960 and 1980—with most of that growth occurring in predominantly white institutions—can also be traced to federal financial aid and the creation of special programs such as TRIO and Upward Bound (Wilson 1987, p. 11). These programs also created many jobs for minority faculty and administrators. Since then, however, funding for many of these fed-

eral programs have been cut.

Reginald Wilson (1987) reports that between 1980 and 1984, the availability of student aid grants as a portion of total financial aid declined from 55 percent to 41 percent. Between 1980 and 1984, available financial aid declined 21 percent in constant dollars, while college tuition rose 11.8 percent (Wilson 1987, p. 12). A study by the College Board found that federal aid to postsecondary students dropped from $22.2 billion to $20.7 billion since 1980 (see *Newsweek on Campus* 1987, p. 16). African-Americans and Hispanics are more likely to require financial aid since they are about twice as likely as whites to be poor (Children's Defense Fund 1989).

Campus-based student aid programs have become increasingly important in addressing the needs of students. For example, the amount of institutional aid to needy undergraduates increased 149 percent since 1979. Since 1979, the number of needy undergraduate students increased from 2.8 million to 3.8 million (*Higher Education and National Affairs* 1987, p. 3).

Expressing a contrary view, William J. Bennett, then Secretary of Education, asserted that federal aid "has not dried up" and that African-American students have equal access to higher education. Rather, Bennett argued that among students with similar achievement levels, African-Americans are just as likely to attend college as whites. Therefore, the problem is "there are too many low performing Black students" with inadequate preparation at the elementary and secondary level. Further, Bennett stated that colleges' retention of students is "not amenable to federal solution" (*Higher Education and National Affairs* 1988, p. 5).

Conclusion

"Anticlimax" may be the best word to describe the status of the now 17-year-old effort to desegregate the faculties of predominantly white colleges and universities. To many observers, affirmative action issues are so complex and compromised that resignation rather than hope follows. The results clearly do not match the expectations (*Change* 1987).

The Carnegie Council on Policy Studies in Higher Education took the position in a 1975 report that affirmative action would take more time to be effective in higher education than the five years that was originally suggested by the federal government. Unfortunately, after three times longer than that recommended time, the impact of affirmative action in terms of increased African-American and Hispanic faculty at predominantly white colleges and universities is still minimal. With an actual decline in the numbers of African-American faculty, and miniscule increases in the numbers of Hispanic faculty, the prospects for diversity look extremely dismal unless the institutions find ways to make affirmative action a reality and not just a rhetorical exercise.

Sudarkasa quickly points out that the majority of African-Americans and Hispanics who have been hired, and who enroll in school, have done so without any special or preferential treatment. In fact, the opposite is true: they do so *in spite of* barriers that they confront at almost every turn (Sudarkasa 1987).

Sudarkasa also mentions that, as a matter of record, the progress of white female faculty as a result of affirmative action has far outstripped that of African-Americans and Hispanics. She explains that this fact is important, not to drive a wedge between minorities and the white women who have benefitted from affirmative action, but to point out that these women are not usually the targets of charges of incompetence or of lawsuits charging reverse discrimination. Rather, the relatively smaller number of African-Americans and Hispanics who have benefited from affirmative action are resented because of beliefs that they received preference without being prepared, and that they profited from "quotas" without being qualified.

Note that the term "quotas" is often viewed as a pejorative label used to dismiss all numerical goals. Since the Bakke case prohibited quotas, while allowing race to be considered, use of that term is thought to be an indicator of antagonism toward affirmative action (see later section).

The higher education community has been running very hard with their affirmative action activities over the past 20 years, yet has stayed in the same place. Now, in a climate much less sympathetic to social inclusion, Wilson (1987) argues that the motivation to promote diversity in higher education must come from a higher sense of national necessity that supersedes the narrow self-interest of faculties and makes a more realistic assessment of the resistance to change.

Given trends in the supply and demand of African-American faculty, what is the likelihood of substantially increasing the level of African-American and Hispanic participation as faculty and administrators in higher education? To Sudarkasa (1987), the answer is clear: In the short run for the country as a whole, the chances are minimal to none. The chances of significantly decreasing the level of that participation is very great if affirmative action policy is abandoned.

On the other hand, Wilson (1987) says that this would, at first glance, seem to be a propitious time for institutions to move toward racial and ethnic parity. The demographics are all favorable. Minorities of college-going age are increasing while the post-World War II baby boom generation is aging. Of those in the professoriat, over 50 percent are estimated to be replaced by the end of the century.

Demand for African-American and Hispanic faculty might increase as a result of the changing composition of the traditional college-age population: The majority of public school students in our major cities are minorities, and they will be overwhelmingly so by the year 2000. The birth rates of African-Americans and Hispanics are the highest among ethnic groups in the United States. Indeed, between 1982 and 1987, the nation's Hispanic population increased 22 percent (*Higher Education and National Affairs* 1987, p. 3). Also, 42 percent of immigrants to the United States are Hispanic. By the year 2010, one-third of the American population and the workforce will be minorities, African-Americans will make up 14 percent, Hispanics nearly 15 percent, and Asians about 5 percent (*Black Issues in Higher Education* 1987, p. 1). By the year 2025, minorities are expected to make up nearly 40 percent of all 18- to 24-year-olds (Mingle 1987a).

Still one cannot help but recognize that the presence of African-Americans and Hispanics in higher education in 1989 falls woefully short of where men and women of good will hoped and trusted it could be (*Change* 1987). The higher education community must heed the warning signals—the statistics on supply and demand, the racial incidents on campuses across the country, and the evidence of growing mistrust between communities.

EFFECTIVE AFFIRMATIVE ACTION:
Institutional Approaches and Barriers

A critical barrier to affirmative action progress is the tendency toward "deferred responsibility," that is, each constituency holding another responsible for failures of initiative or implementation. Administrators are perceived by their critics as committed to slow, hierarchical progress; faculty as tradition-bound and ideologically resistant; students as distracted or unrealistic. All of these perceptions may be accurate, but together they seem to weaken the collective spirit and paralyze the collective effort necessary for successful affirmative action (Ohio State University 1985).

In this chapter, the following institutional approaches and strategies that can overcome the barrier of deferred responsibility are examined:
- Institutional leadership.
- The faculty.
- African-American and Hispanic members of the academic community.
- Search committees.
- Affirmative action offices.
- Special recruitment programs and activities.

Examples of effective affirmative action practices within U.S. colleges and universities are presented. A more extensive case study is presented on the African-American presence at Antioch College.

High visibility and determined leadership by the chief executive and academic officers of the college or university are the most important elements . . . for successful affirmative action.

Institutional Leadership

High visibility and determined leadership by the chief executive and academic officers of the college or university are the most important elements that sets the stage for successful affirmative action. Dimensions of the leadership variable are values and priorities, leadership style, behavior and stability. Strong leaders are perceived as personally committed to affirmative action; to treat affirmative action as an important institutional priority with resources and staff; to closely monitor decisions and to hold decision-makers accountable; to provide effective two-way communication; and to offer incentives for affirmative action efforts and results (Hyer 1985, Ohio State University 1985).

One criterion in selecting or reappointing vice presidents, deans, and chairs should be the level of effort and results demonstrated in affirmative action. These leaders should be alert to opportunities to hire candidates from target groups.

The administrator must be prepared on occasion to upset people where affirmative action advocacy is concerned.

There are many ways in which chief academic officers can show their support for affirmative action. They can:

- Highlight the institution's affirmative action efforts and successes in public speeches and in meetings with faculty and staff on campus.
- Become aware of departments in which minority faculty are underutilized, and question hirings and promotions in those departments.
- Take advantage of opportunities to appoint or nominate African-Americans and Hispanics to committees or for leadership positions.
- Meet with community leaders and lobbying groups to engage their assistance in recruiting applicants for employment.
- Support professional development programs on campus designed to heighten sensitivity to affirmative action and to improve administrative and supervisory skills (see VanderWaerdt 1982).

Faculty Responses to Affirmative Action

Administrative leadership is crucial but it can be constrained by the norms of academic institutions, particularly departmental autonomy and academic freedom. Academic administrators can exercise leadership based on their positions in the hierarchy, but they should try to maintain consensus and collegial relations within their institutions. These academic norms contrast with the norms in other institutions—for example, with military institutions where the tradition of hierarchy made the entry of women into military academies easier to accomplish despite opposition from military officials (see Exum 1983).

Prior to the enactment of the Civil Rights Act of 1964, amended in 1972 to apply to educational institutions, college and university leaders seemed to support the fight against discrimination and voiced little opposition to the passage of the amendment (VanderWaerdt 1982). Subsequently, however, many institutions and academicians resisted changes in their procedures and practices that would have actively encouraged African-Americans and Hispanics to be considered for faculty and administrative positions.

The early 1970s brought numerous articles decrying the

amendment as a threat to academic standards, and predicting that vast numbers of unqualified women and minorities would have to be hired to comply with government regulations (refer to Loftus 1977). Another perspective is that discrimination causes less qualified people to be hired because significant groups of qualified people are not considered for positions. Moreover, the fact is that hiring less qualified candidates because of race or sex is a violation of the law (VanderWaerdt 1982).

There is little credible evidence of strong faculty commitment toward affirmative action in faculty hiring, manifested behaviorally in vigorous recruitment. Rather, some faculty have advanced an intellectual, ideological argument that affirmative action results in reverse discrimination, lowered standards, unfair quotas, and disincentives for excellence. A college or university committed to excellence, some still say, can only afford to commit itself to nondiscrimination, as distinct from affirmative action, in faculty recruitment and retention.

The persistent notion that affirmative action threatens academic quality has been widely addressed. First and foremost, vigorous affirmative action has been shown repeatedly to enhance rather than threaten research excellence by enlarging the range and sharpening the rigor of inquiry. In such disciplines as history, political science, and literary theory, African-American and Hispanic scholars have advanced the frontier of knowledge by exploring new areas and, in some notable instances, by producing methodological innovations that reshape the discipline. Yet, many minority scholars perceive that it is a professional risk for them to study ethnic issues, and that the work of minority scholars in these areas is not recognized (Valverde 1980). In some instances, it is possible to question whether passive resistance to affirmative action is not also a resistance to variety, innovation, and progress in the discipline—as when African-American and Hispanic scholars are told that their expertise is not academically respectable and thus in itself is a threat to research excellence (Ohio State University 1985).

Resistance to affirmative action based on meritocratic values appears to be neutral, objective, competitive, and fair. A meritocracy is considered appropriate because of the view that any remaining discrimination in hiring or mobility is a remnant of the past and does not reflect actual, ongoing operations (Oliver and Glick 1982). Yet the reality is that neutrality and objectivity are often absent from hiring deliberations, and thus, do not protect minorities against discrimination. In practice, a "patronage merit system" exists in higher education which values both achievement and performance as well as personal style, conforming behavior, and mentors and sponsors. This system is closed to many African-Americans and Hispanics because of differences in racial, cultural, research, or social class backgrounds.

Adherence to the presumed meritocracy serves to disguise the character and imperfections of the merit system while legitimizing the exclusion of African-American and Hispanic faculty (Exum 1983). This view can also serve to burden or victimize individual African-American and Hispanic faculty whose presence may be shrouded by arguments that pit academic excellence against affirmative action.

The literature corroborates the personal experiences of the authors which suggest that minority scholars and their white colleagues simply see the academic environment differently. A tremendous gap in perceptions often exists between these groups because of the inability of white faculty to hear the voices of the African-American and Hispanic scholars. For example, in studies of African-American and white faculty, white faculty were of the opinion that "Blacks were doing better than ever" while African-American faculty perceived tremendous obstacles in gaining tenure and promotion (Staples and Jones 1984). Another study found that African-American faculty felt that their research institution was "racist" while simultaneously acknowledging that a positive racial climate existed at the departmental level and that the criteria for tenure and promotion were universally applied without regard to race (Elmore and Blackburn 1983).

The important underlying point in Elmore and Blackburn is that these African-American faculty members were favorably disposed toward their departments, but less favorably disposed toward the university at large. The most virulent racism in these institutions may very well be located in the departments where there are no African-American or Hispanic faculty members.

Again, a distinction must be made between the articulation of the general cultural value of social equality and the reality of specific situations. Staples and Jones (1984) observe that because racial identity and racial inequality coexist with national values of equality and a color-blind society, maintaining the social order depends on the perceptions of meritocracy and internal locus of control. Thus, whereas minority faculty perceive barriers to the meritocracy based on their personal and group experiences, members of the majority group rest comfortably assured that the meritocracy is effectively operational.

Advocacy by African-American and Hispanic Members of the Academic Community

Advocacy by members of the target groups is second only to strong institutional leadership in affirmative action (Hyer 1985). Many successful affirmative action programs are the outgrowth of advocacy and leadership by campus advocates. Activity by African-Americans and Hispanics already on campus can provide crucial support to locating and attracting candidates. Thus, attention must be given to retaining and promoting African-Americans and Hispanics already in the university community. This attention has other benefits as well; the lack of role models for students has been frequently cited as a factor in the difficulty of recruiting and retaining minority students (see previous section).

Coalition activity by African-Americans, Hispanics, and whites on campus can be effective when these advocates target central administrative leaders, have two to three senior minority faculty playing leadership roles, and provide support by locating candidates. Clearly there must be simultaneous cooperative effort among various campus constituencies, but an important leadership function can be played by these groups.

Search Committees

Since the search committee is a standard tool for screening and interviewing candidates, it can facilitate or serve as a barrier to affirmative action effectiveness (see Goodwin 1975). Thus, the composition, work activities, and attitudes of search committees are important. Search committees should consist of people whose personal commitment to affirmative action gives them the time, energy, and inclination to explore minority networks when particular vacancies occur, and to introduce candidates to their target group peers on the occasion of the campus interviews.

In many ways, employment practices affecting faculty have not substantially changed from the "old boy" network before the Civil Rights Act of 1964. For example, although there has been a substantial increase in ads placed in *The Chronicle of Higher Education* since the 1972 *Higher Education Guidelines for Affirmative Action*, and three-quarters of institutions do advertise nationally, there has been little substantial change in the sex or race of new hires. Indeed, about one-third of the positions were filled internally. The federal regulations of 1972 have not resulted in substantial increases in new hires of different ethnic groups, but have resulted in increased costs (Dingerson, Rodman, and Wade 1982; Socolow 1978; Wisenhunt 1980).

The effective affirmative action search process should have the following features:

- Flexibility in defining subspecialty and academic rank of new openings if such redefinition increases access to a larger pool of applicants.
- Search committee members who have a personal commitment to affirmative action and who are willing to take the extra time to recruit more aggressively, i.e., more phone calls, letters, etc.
- A personalized touch in which candidates are notified of search progress, applications are acknowledged, personal follow-ups occur, and sensitivity to candidates styles or postures are incorporated.
- Timely offers to candidates since some candidates from targeted populations in some disciplines may be highly sought after.
- Inclusion of unsolicited applications or inquiries.
- Reliance on prevalent professional files, registries, and data banks to identify candidates from targeted populations who have received significant grants or recognition.
- The use of contacts in organizations, associations, and agencies that conduct job searches to tap into the personal networks among members of targeted populations in appropriate fields (Ohio State University 1985).

Aggressive affirmative action search techniques can include the following:

- Broad advertising covering a range of journals and job registries specifically geared to target populations.
- The use of all available professional occasions (conferences, consultations, etc.) to actually solicit curricula vitae from promising candidates in targeted populations.

- The creation and continually updating of departmental files or talent banks prior to a particular faculty vacancy.
- The solicitation of advice and counsel from continuing faculty who are members of targeted populations.
- The use of alumni from targeted populations.
- Contacts with faculty at predominantly African-American or Hispanic colleges for referrals.
- Contracts with the professional and scholarly societies of target groups as well as members of targeted populations holding professional positions in independent research institutions, industry, government, etc. (Murray 1984, Ohio State University 1985).

Vitae banks are frequently being developed as a means to identify available minority candidates. The actual success of vitae banks, however, is mixed. This resource can be used cynically as a means to collect names to throw into an affirmative action pool without attention to the quality of the credentials. The success of vitae banks "is only as good as the sincerity and commitment of the institutions using them" (Wilson 1987, p. 14).

Academic departments should be encouraged by a variety of rewards and sanctions to increase their representation of targeted groups. Units that have been identified as requiring special attention in faculty recruitment should collaborate with the affirmative action officer in formulating realistic goals and plans. Sometimes the problem may be a small availability pool, in which case the affirmative action officer may be able to assist the office in developing more aggressive search committee techniques, in securing additional budgetary flexibility, or in formulating plans to increase the pool through expansion of graduate or postgraduate training opportunities. Sometimes a particular unit may exhibit a low level of effort in affirmative action recruitment in which case the affirmative action officer might be able to suggest specific and often simple strategies for intensifying the effort, including rewards for successful effort in the form of additional authorized positions or other budgetary incentives (Ohio State University 1985).

In no case should inadequate search and recruitment procedures be allowed to persist. The affirmative action officer should regularly monitor search procedures in departments with a prior history of weak effort. In cases where inadequate procedures remain uncorrected, the affirmative action officer should recommend to the dean and provost the same types of sanctions now used for inadequate performance in teaching, research, and service (Ohio State University 1985).

Two final observations: First, the issue of tokenism must be addressed and steps taken to prevent it. Research indicates that there is now an increasing trend toward giving out a small proportion of positions reserved for targeted populations and then abandoning the pursuit of such candidates for future vacancies, regardless of the number of future vacancies (Finkelstein 1983).

In this way, white women and African-American or Hispanic candidates are sometimes placed in a position to compete with each other for the same affirmative action position— effectively limiting the total number of minorities who are eventually hired. Caution may be advisable to avoid using affirmative action as an exclusive, rather than inclusive, vehicle for faculty hiring.

Finally, when African-American or Hispanic candidates are invited to campus for an interview, they must be treated with the respect accorded to other candidates. A commonly stated perception among minority academics is that they are invited to interviews as a type of "window dressing," but their position as a viable candidate is not taken seriously. In this way, search committees extend interviews as a means of demonstrating that the pool of candidates has been inclusive. Indeed, the mixed or ambiguous signals that minorities may perceive while on campus visits may lead some of them to refuse job offers even if they are made (see Exum 1983).

Affirmative Action Offices

Affirmative action advocacy must reflect the mission and purposes of the institution in order to be effective. This definition of effectiveness, however, is not normative practice. With some exceptions, affirmative action offices focus on compliance and on responding to goals and timetables established by others instead of generating goals based on institutional commitments. Thus, if institution-wide advances are made, they are primarily passive responses to imposed federal guidelines.

Over the past 17 years, universities have shown a clear lack of significant progress in affirmative action, but the universities have consistently been found to be in compliance with federal guidelines. Any pride which universities take in being models of compliance can no longer obscure the performance gap between meeting federal guidelines and achieving genuine equal opportunity within the academic community (Ohio State University 1985).

Yet, an advocacy role is not without risk. Court decisions have backed the right of employers to take disciplinary action against the affirmative action officer who takes the advocate route and files suit on behalf of employees (Fortunata 1985).

Effective affirmative action advocacy will require that the affirmative action officers are recognized as key administrative leaders rather than peripheral monitors of compliance activities. Affirmative action officers must be in a position to influence policies before they are made, not simply to review them after the fact (Stetson 1984).

All university administrators should be held directly accountable to the affirmative action officer for acceptable effort—and eventual success—through the same budgetary and personnel rewards and sanctions by which they are now held accountable for discharging their other responsibilities.

The affirmative action officer should report directly to the chief executive or academic officer of the college or university and should be the president's staff associate on key university bodies, such as the board of trustees, the deans, admissions, and the university senate. A direct reporting line not only allows the affirmative action officer to operate from a position of strength, but is also logical, as affirmative action issues cut across organizational levels and must be perceived as a high-level institutional commitment (Ohio State University 1985).

Affirmative action advocacy requires that the office perform several functions (see Ohio State University 1985, Vander-Waerdt 1982). These offices must:

- Conduct systematic advocacy and collaborative goal setting through regular advice and counsel with individual administrative units and policy committees.
- Advise and counsel appropriate administrators on the rewards for acceptable levels of effort in meeting agreed-upon goals and on sanctions for unacceptable levels of effort.
- Continually review all college and university policies for their impact on equity for faculty from targeted groups. No new policy or standard should be instituted without prior consultation with the affirmative action office.
- Plan educational programming that includes regular seminars, workshops, and training sessions on affirmative

action issues for all university constituencies.

- Publish and distribute a brief and readable internal annual report. Interpretations of statistics on recruitment, retention, and harassment rather than on the mere cataloguing of data should be emphasized.
- Create and maintain the necessary data profiles and statistics on students, staff, and faculty who are members of the various discriminated groups to identify problems and monitor progress.
- Develop and coordinate both formal and informal affirmative action-related grievance procedures that earn the trust and respect of staff, students, faculty, and administrators.

The most successful programs occur when affirmative action officers are clear about their roles and make conscious decisions on the division of responsibilities and issues of representation. Some affirmative action officers are not able to withstand the pressure of their peer groups; some are overzealous and counterproductive. Some have conflicts with the personnel officer due to differences in approaches to problem-solving. If the chief academic officer serves as the affirmative action officer—which is not an uncommon arrangement—a conflict of interest may occur if that person is not strongly committed to the vigorous pursuit of equality. Whatever arrangement is used, it is imperative that the affirmative action officer has a clear vision of realistic goals, timetables, and results, and can serve as an advocate to meet these objectives.

A candid view of a president's perspective of affirmative action officers was given by Kenneth E. Wright, president of Passiac County Community College, to a meeting of the New Jersey Association of Affirmative Action in Higher Education. Wright told the affirmative action officers that "if you really want to be effective, come to us with solutions and not problems . . . .We really get tired of the bad news and all of the problems. We'll be much more responsive when we are approached from a positive viewpoint" (*Black Issues in Higher Education* 1988, p. 9).

Special Recruitment Programs and Activities
This discussion of the availability pool, the limited demand for African-American and Hispanic faculty, and graduate school enrollments make it clear that increasing the proportion of African-American and Hispanic faculty will require more than

simply increasing the number of Ph.D.s. The current status of African-American and Hispanic faculty is not likely to be remedied through traditional means such as the regulation-compliance approaches which dominate affirmative action policy in higher education.

New ideas and innovative approaches are necessary to develop, recruit, and retain African-American and Hispanic professors. These approaches can include curriculum review, incentives to minority graduate students, and support for elementary and secondary students.

Curriculum Review

Curriculum review can be critical to the hiring process. There may be a need for careful evaluation of the curriculum and a deliberate assessment of future employment needs. Consideration should be given to ways of strengthening the curriculum to attract more African-American and Hispanic scholars (Stetson 1984). For example, the Temple University Board of Trustees approved a 10-year academic plan to triple African-American faculty partly by strengthening African-American studies and establishing a center for African-American culture and history (*Black Issues in Higher Education* 1986).

Kean College of Union, New Jersey is also seeking to meet the challenge of diversity through curriculum reform. In the 1970s Kean initiated a program in which students could enroll in the first two years of their curriculum in Spanish concurrently with their in English-as-a-second-language courses. Kean employed 23 Hispanic faculty members in 1987, most of whom taught courses other than Spanish. The core curriculum courses also included focus on diversity (*Black Issues in Higher Education* 1987, pp. 1–5).

Incentives to Graduate Students

One response to the dwindling pool of potential African-American and Hispanic professors is for institutions to "grow" their own. Some institutions have had moderate success in identifying disciplines in which minorities are underrepresented, by recruiting doctoral candidates into those areas, and hiring them as junior faculty when they complete their studies. Washington University in St. Louis and Wayne State University have used this approach. Ohio State University leads the nation in producing minority Ph.D.s (Wilson 1987, p. 144).

Other colleges and universities have come together with industry to form consortia to promote access in higher education. Several consortia—the National Consortium for Educational Access in Athens, Georgia; the National Consortium for Graduate Degrees in Engineering (GEM) at Notre Dame, Indiana; and the Consortium for Graduate Study in Management in St. Louis, Missouri—provide financial support for study at nationally known graduate and professional programs as well as on-the-job training and employment opportunities. Since 1976, GEM has accumulated 400 alumni; in 1986, 85 students received doctorates (*Black Issues in Higher Education* 1987).

In another joint effort, Oberlin, Williams, Mount Holyoke, and Carleton Colleges began a research scholar program to encourage minority students to consider careers in college or university teaching. Funded by a grant from the Ford Foundation, each of the four colleges selects four to six students each year to participate in the program. Each student receives financial support and collaborates on research projects with designated faculty mentors (Burch 1988, p. 6).

Also receiving high praise is the Black Doctoral Fellowship Program of the Florida Endowment Fund for Higher Education, previously known as the McKnight Black Doctoral Fellowship Programs. This program provides $15,000 in annual support to each of 25 African-American students attending doctorate-granting institutions in Florida. The program emphasizes study in the arts and sciences, business, and engineering.

The success of the program, which began in 1984, has been immediate, according to its executive director, Israel Tribble. By fall 1987, the Florida Program had sponsored 92 fellows, many of whom would have been passed over by other graduate programs because their GRE scores range from 640 to 1450 and average 940, not the 1,000 typically required. Yet the students are excelling in competitive programs.

To many observers, the success of these programs indicates that the potential of African-American students cannot be predicted by test-taking skills. Indeed, while Florida's public institutions have produced one African-American engineering Ph.D. in the last five years, the McKnight program is now sponsoring 11 students in engineering programs. The seven fellows in computer science doctorate programs exceeds the total number of doctorates awarded to African-Americans throughout the United States in that field in 1987 (*Black Issues in Higher Education* 1987, p 8).

In other initiatives, several state legislatures, for example in Connecticut, Michigan, and New Jersey, have made money available for new graduate fellowships. New Jersey's Minority Academic Career program is seen as a model because it forgives students one-quarter of their loans for each year they teach in the state after receiving their degree. In this way, they encourage and support professorial career choices (*Chronicle of Higher Education* 1987, p. 24).

Similarly in 1987 the California State University System began a program to help women and minorities get their doctorates and increase the number of women and minority faculty members on system campuses. The program provides up to $30,000 for doctoral study which is "forgiven" if the recipients work within the university system for at least five years (*Black Issues in Higher Education* 1988, p. 8).

The Ford Foundation and the National Research Council sponsor programs to assist minority scholars at both the predoctoral and postdoctoral stages. These programs join such well established efforts as the Department of Education's Graduate Professional Opportunities Program and those sponsored by the National Science Foundation (NSF) in such fields as environmental biology and engineering.

NSF began its Minority Graduate Fellowship Program in 1978 to increase the number of minority scientists, mathematicians, and engineers. Between 1978 and 1988, NSF received 4,486 applications and made 548 awards (National Science Foundation 1988).

These special financial aid and recruiting activities have been instituted to ensure the broadest and most diverse pool of professorial candidates possible. These opportunities offer African-American and Hispanic scholars important mentor relationships and "grooms" them to achieve excellence.

In their book, *American Professors: A National Resource Imperiled*, Howard R. Bowen and Jack H. Schuster (1986), call for a wide-ranging national fellowship program to identify and support minority students interested in academic careers. "Unless this is done," they write, "affirmative action policies, even if carried out in good faith by campuses, will be inadequate to prevent serious erosion in the numbers and quality of minorities in the academic profession." Yet no such pro-

The success of these programs indicates that the potential of African-American students cannot be predicted by test-taking skills.

gram has been created and affirmative action officers widely bemoan the lack of national leadership on the matter.

Support for Elementary and
Secondary School Students

Harold Hodgkinsons's (1985) report, *All One System*, emphasized that educational opportunities at all levels from kindergarten through graduate school should be considered as "all one system." Implied in this perspective is that significant increases in the pool of perspective African-American and Hispanic faculty members will only occur by supporting students in the primary and secondary schools.

Indeed, a summary report of 33 states' programs to recruit and retrain minorities in higher education shows that states have put great emphasis on collaborative work with the schools to improve academic preparation (Mingle 1987a, 1987b). For example, deficiencies in elementary and secondary programs in Chicago are said to have contributed to local students' poor college performance (*Higher Education and National Affairs* 1988, p. 5). However, states use a wide variety of approaches to minority participation in higher education; critics charge that the lack of consistency across states works to the detriment of minorities (*Black Issues in Higher Education* 1986, p. 6).

In 1987, Ohio State University (OSU) proposed a comprehensive affirmative action plan consistent with Hodgkinson's ideas. To create a larger pool of college-eligible African-American students, Ohio State University plans to create The Young Scholars program, which will target sixth-graders from urban Ohio areas who would not ordinarily have the opportunity, aspirations, or support to attend college. Students accepted into the program will be admitted to the university and provided financial aid if they complete a college preparatory curriculum, participate in summer programs at OSU, and maintain satisfactory academic progress. When fully implemented, 400 sixth-graders will be initiated each spring (*Black Issues in Higher Education* 1987, pp. 1, 6).

In a similar effort, the University of the District of Columbia initiated precollege programs in 1982 with its Saturday Academy for eighth grade students and teachers. A special Science and Engineering Program, funded by the National Aeronautics and Space Administration, provided training in mathematics, computer science, and electrical engineering skills to more than 300 students and 40 teachers in 1986 (*Black Issues in Higher Education* 1987, p. 9).

In a 10-year plan to increase the number of African-American engineering students at Florida A & M University, the university has established a precollege recruitment plan targeted for African-American fourth-graders. The plan includes a Saturday Academy for elementary school students in 10 cities, an engineering training project for seventh-through ninth-graders, and summer programs for high school students (*Black Issues in Higher Education* 1987, p. 9).

Similarly, in 1987 Bryn Mawr College received a grant from the GTE Foundation for a two-year pilot program designed to encourage 30 scientifically gifted African-American and Hispanic young women from Philadelphia high schools to pursue careers in the sciences. Mentorship with successful minority women scientists is a high priority of that program (*Black Issues in Higher Education* 1987, p. 10).

In 1987, Xavier University became the first private university in the country to adopt a sixth-grade public school class and guarantee them tuition assistance. The school in which the class was adopted had a minority population of 98 percent. The College Opportunity Program being offered to support the students' success included mentoring, tutoring, and academic enrichment (*Black Issues in Higher Education* 1987, p. 17).

Examples of Effective Affirmative Action Practices

To assist colleges and universities in improving their affirmative action practices, the American Council on Education recently published a handbook proposing strategies to reduce the trend of declining minority participation in higher education. The first of its kind, the handbook covers faculty, students, administrators, campus climate, teaching and learning, and the curriculum. The handbook also profiles three institutions—The University of Massachusetts at Boston, Miami-Dade Community College, and Mount St. Mary's College in California—that have made sustained efforts to increase the role of minorities on their campuses (Green 1989).

Several colleges and universities have had successful faculty recruitment plans. A frequently cited example is Miami University of Ohio. Gary Hunter, the affirmative action officer, states that the successful recruitment and employment strategies have as their cornerstone the uncompromising leadership of the university president. Also important is the active involvement of the academic leadership such as deans and chairs, including the imposition of occasional sanctions. Hunter explains the affirmative action philosophy as expecting a department to hire minority faculty and graduate minority students. "If a department is not hiring or graduating minorities, they're in trouble" stated Hunter (*Black Issues in Higher Education* 1988, p. 9).

Another institution, the University of Massachusetts at Boston, also aggressively recruits African-American faculty. Eight percent of their faculty is African-American, of which 5.5 percent have tenure (Garza 1988, p. 119).

There are other examples of effective affirmative action ideas:

- Virginia Tech University's Committee on Equal Opportunity and Affirmative Action has given affirmative action awards for four years to individuals who have shown exceptional commitment (*Black Issues in Higher Education* 1987, p. 8).

- In 1988 the University of Wisconsin-Madison launched a minority recruitment and retention plan expected to double the number of entering minority students in the next five years and add more than 200 new minority faculty and staff in the next three years. The plan includes several components: student orientation and counseling; outreach to local schools; scholarships for undergraduate and graduate students; faculty and staff minority recruitment; an ethnic studies credit requirement for all undergraduate students; the creation of a multicultural center; and strong written policies, programs, and procedures to deal with discrimination or harassment by students and employees. The plan guarantees that no student will incur a debt of more than $800 a year or need to borrow at all in the first year (*Higher Education and National Affairs* 1988, p. 4).

- The Bucknell University approved a three-part affirmative action plan in 1988 to increase the number of minority and women faculty. The plan will create extra faculty positions for minorities in two ways: by linking the hiring of women and minorities to a designated number of permanent tenure-track positions and by allowing more time for faculty searches. Two "floating" faculty positions will be created to allow departments in the science and engineering departments to begin searches three years before faculty members retire (*Higher Education and National Affairs* 1988, p. 4).

- At the Massachusetts Institute of Technology, each department chair keeps an updated list of minority graduate students in a discipline and keeps in touch with them. Each chair maintains an active network with faculty at other institutions, with graduate students, and with post-doctoral fellows (Green 1989).
- The University of Kansas has a Langston Hughes Visiting Professorship that brings a succession of exemplary professors to the campus (Green 1989).
- The Florida Endowment Fund offers a junior faculty development fellowship program to provide teaching and research assistance to women and minorities who work in disciplines in which they are underrepresented. Twenty $15,000 fellowships are awarded annually; 72 fellowships have been awarded since 1984 (Green 1989).
- In 1984 the University of California established the president's fellowship program, which offers postdoctoral fellowships to minority and women students for academic appointments for major research institutions (Green 1989).
- Five or more full-time research appointments are offered by the Carolina Minority Postdoctoral Scholars Program at the University of North Carolina at Chapel Hill (Green 1989).
- To increase underrepresented minority faculty on the campus of the University of Illinois at Urbana-Champaign, postdoctoral fellowships are offered for one academic year (Green 1989).
- Williams College encourages minority Ph.D. candidates to pursue careers in college teaching through a fellowship program that supports the completion of their dissertations and provides the opportunity to teach one course (Green 1989).
- In 1985 the Ford Foundation and the National Research Council announced a $9-million fellowship program to support 120 minority doctoral students over a five-year period (*Chronicle of Higher Education* 1986, p. 24).

Most of these initiatives involve crucial components of success: financial support, and opportunities to be mentored or to pursue research interests. These variables specifically address the barriers commonly identified for African-American and Hispanic faculty (see previous section).

Advocacy strategies for faculty recruitment also include such measures as providing funds to hire nationally established scholars from targeted populations at senior levels or endowing several chairs across the university reserved for eminent scholars whose research focuses on the target populations (The Ohio State University 1985).

Case Study: The African-American Presence at Antioch College

A comparison of the status of African-American students and faculty at Antioch College and in the United States reveals both extraordinary exceptions and parallels in affirmative action history. Antioch College is a national liberal arts college with several distinctive traditions: the integration of work and study, community government, and a focus on the individual's development of his/her personal values and life philosophy.

Based in Yellow Springs, Ohio, Antioch has played an important role in higher education since its founding in 1852. Its first president, Horace Mann, was the architect of public schooling in the United States and a leader in supporting higher education for women. Antioch was one of the first nonsectarian colleges in the country.

In the Antioch educational model, students are expected to reach beyond conventional learning, partly through alternating work and study experiences. An Antioch education is expected to enable students to take risks in order to test values and their career choices. Antioch's long tradition of community governance encourages active problem-solving, conflict resolution, reflection, and collaboration.

African-American Students

Antioch College was a notable exception to the racial exclusionary practices which characterized higher education between 1876 and 1900. Antioch was not yet founded in 1823 when the first African-American college graduate, Alexander Lucius, completed his studies at Middlebury College. However, after its founding in 1852, Antioch was still one of the first colleges in the United States to admit African-Americans. The first African-American Antioch graduate, Alfred Hampton, completed his studies in 1888.

From 1970 to 1977, African-American enrollment in higher

education nearly doubled, but was still 25 to 30 percent below parity. After 1977, African-American enrollment increases leveled off; in the 1980s enrollment began to decline.

The pattern of African-American enrollment at Antioch College since 1976 has mirrored the national pattern. It is important to point out, however, that between 1980 and 1984, African-American enrollment at Antioch far exceeded the average African-American enrollment at other four-year institutions. Still, African-American enrollment at Antioch in 1988 has declined to its 1976 level, and it remains well below the proportion of African-American high school graduates in the nation (see Table 5). On a national level, the major declines for African-American students are occurring in four-year colleges (like Antioch) and for first-time, full-time freshmen in both two-year and four-year colleges.

TABLE 5

PERCENTAGE ENROLLMENT OF AFRICAN-AMERICAN STUDENTS IN FOUR-YEAR INSTITUTIONS OF HIGHER EDUCATION IN THE USA AND AT ANTIOCH COLLEGE

	1976	1978	1980	1982	1984	1986	1988
USA Four-Year Institutions*	8.5	8.5	8.5	8.3	8.0	7.9	Not Available
Antioch	8.4	8.2	11.0	13.1	10.6	8.8	8.5

Source: 7th Annual Status Report on Minorities in Higher Education. Reprinted by permission.

*Calculations by Cecilia Ottinger of ACE.

African-American Faculty

Professor Walter Anderson became Antioch's first African-American faculty member when he joined the music department in 1946. At that time, out of 3,000 African-Americans who listed college teacher as their occupation, only 78 had *ever* taught at a predominantly white school (some of them were not full-time faculty).

African-American faculty hiring at Antioch since the 1940s has generally exceeded national averages for all institutions and for predominantly white colleges (see Table 6). The proportion of African-American faculty in the United States since

1975 has been less than 5 percent overall and less than 2.5 percent at predominantly white institutions.

The African-American faculty presence at Antioch in this period has ranged from about 2 percent to its current level of 12 percent. However, the general pattern of African-American faculty hiring at Antioch College has been uneven

TABLE 6

TIMELINE OF AFRICAN-AMERICAN FACULTY PRESENCE IN THE USA AND AT ANTIOCH COLLEGE

YEAR	ANTIOCH (a)		USA		
	N	%	N	%	DESCRIPTION
1776 to 1940	Virtually no African-American faculty at white institutions				(b)
1941	0	0	2	-	Tenured in white institutions (j)
1946	1	-	78	-	Who had ever taught in a white institution, even part-time (c)
1958	3	3.5	200	-	In white institutions (c)
1961	3	2.7	300	-	In white institutions (d)
1968	3	2.0		2.2	In all institutions (d,e)
1972	15	9.4		2.9	In all institutions (d,e)
1975	6	4.3		4.4	In all institutions (h)
1976	7	7.7		4.4	In all institutions (d)
1977	5	5.1		4.4	In all institutions (f,h)
				4.3	In all four-year state institutions (g)
1979	2	3.3		4.4	In all institutions (d)
1981	3	5.2		4.2	In all institutions (i)
1983	1	1.9		4.0	In all institutions (f)
1985	3	5.1		4.1	In all institutions (f)
1987	4	5.0			Data not available
1988	7	12.3			Data not available

Notes:
a. Data drawn from the Antioch College personnel files. All nembers reflect full-time faculty.
b. Weinberg 1977, p. 9.
c. Ebony 1947, p. 16.
d. Exum 1983, p. 385.
e. "All" includes both predominately Black and historically white institutions. African-American faculty at white institutions are, at most, half of the total.
f. Green 1989, p. 81-82; ACE 1988, p. 32.
g. Franklin 1987, p. 5.
h. Reed 1983, p. 335.
i. Sudarkasa 1987, p. 4.
j. Garza 1988, p. 19.

and reflects the national pattern of declines. Moreover, six of the seven African-American faculty at Antioch have been hired since 1987, and there is cause for concern about retention; only one African-American faculty member has tenure, and four are on nontenure track appointments. Of the seven African-American faculty members, five are assistant professors, one is an associate professor, and one is a full professor. They teach in a variety of disciplines including chemistry, philosophy, education, psychology, social work/law, and cooperative education, unlike the national concentration in education.

Findings and Conclusions

At specific points in time, Antioch College approached numerical parity in both African-American student enrollment and African-American faculty hiring—accomplishments that the nation as a whole has not yet attained. Recent affirmative action successes at Antioch can be attributed to many factors. Administrative leadership committed to affirmative action goals was a key variable in focusing attention on the issue. A strong and vigorous multiracial group of campus advocates (both students and faculty) worked with search committees to network with professional organizations, and to locate and give personal attention to minority candidates. Antioch's tradition of excellence and its historical legacy of equity also invoked an important sense of mission, as well as a sense of the importance of diversity.

Most experts in higher education predict many faculty vacancies in the 1990s; Antioch College also anticipates the creation of about 20 new faculty positions in the next four years; the college is challenged to strengthen and maintain its recent progress toward racial diversity. Both the nation and Antioch College have demonstrated that rapid increases can be achieved with commitment and perseverance. It has been done before—it can be done again in the 1990s.

NATIONAL RESPONSES TO AFFIRMATIVE ACTION ISSUES IN HIGHER EDUCATION

Affirmative action programs in colleges and universities can be affected by situations and circumstances that occur outside of the particular campus. Court decisions, government agencies, public commissions, and professional associations have all had varying degrees of impact on affirmative action. Because affirmative action in higher education is an issue that generates significant emotion and heated responses by supporters and opponents alike, it is not simply an isolated institutional phenomenon. Rather, it is closely watched, and both supporters and opponents have been active in trying to bring external influences to bear so that the outcome of the program is in line with their own desires and expectations.

Under Title VII of the 1964 Civil Rights Act, 11 African-American faculty members have sued for problems related to alleged tenure discrimination; none has been successful.

Court Decisions

A significant source of external pressure for colleges and universities has been the federal court system. In a 1971 case, *Griggs v. Duke Power Company,* the federal courts made it illegal to discriminate by using hiring selection methods which systematically disadvantage minorities. The courts consistently upheld affirmative action in 1979 and 1980 (*Weber v. Kaiser Aluminum* and *Fullilove v. Khutznick*) (see Exum 1983, p. 389).

Specific challenges to affirmative action plans in faculty hiring have been heard by the court. In *Valentine v. Smith* (1981), the U.S. Court of Appeals held that a predominantly white state institution's decision to hire an African-American, rather than a white candidate, in order to meet affirmative action goals was constitutional (Reed 1983, p. 345).

Many white males have opposed affirmative action because they feel it discriminates against them. The first significant court case that was heard on the basis that affirmative action is actually reverse discrimination against white males was *DeFunis v. the University of Washington* (O'Neil 1975). Marco DeFunis had applied for admission to the university's law school and was turned down. In 1971, a court ruled in favor of DeFunis and granted him admission because the law school had a preferential admissions program at the time which considered the minority status of those applicants. But, when the Washington State Supreme Court reversed the trial judge's decision in 1973, which in effect upheld affirmative action, it pointedly noted that "If minorities are to live within the rule of law, they must enjoy equal representation within our legal system" (O'Neil 1975, p. 15). The case was appealed to the U.S. Supreme Court, which refused to hear it because by that time DeFunis had graduated from law school, so the issue was moot. Even though this case has no relation to faculty hiring, it did establish the point that race could be taken into account in a selection process.

A similar case is that of *Alan Bakke v. the Regents of the University of California.* Alan Bakke, also a white male, had applied to the medical school at the University of California at Davis, and had been turned down in 1973 and 1974. In the years that Bakke sought admission, 2,600 and 3,700 applications were received for the 100 places in each class, 16 of which had been set aside for disadvantaged students, most of whom were nonwhite, and some of whom had lower grades and test scores than Bakke. Alleging that he had been screened out because of his race, Bakke sued, and both the trial court and California Supreme Court agreed with him, ruling that the admission program was improper. Upon review of the case in 1978, the U.S. Supreme Court ruled that while Bakke's admission was appropriate, race could indeed be taken into account as one factor in the overall admissions process. However, the court outlawed programs that set aside a specific number of places for minorities.

This "half-a-loaf" decision had something in it for the supporters and the opponents of affirmative action, and thus is viewed as ushering in a decade of ambiguity. It allowed affirmative action programs to continue, but hardly gave them a ringing endorsement (Simmons 1982). The opinion written by Justice Lewis F. Powell, Jr.—believed to have established the ground rules for most college affirmative action programs for students ever since—said that educators should decide how much weight to give to race in admissions decision (*The Chronicle of Higher Education* 1988, p. A14). The Bakke decision did not directly address the particular issue of faculty recruitment, nor it did contain any statements that would prohibit the predominantly white institutions from recruiting African-American or Hispanic faculty in a specific, purposeful fashion.

Another more categorical suit had been filed in 1970 by the National Association for the Advancement of Colored People's (NAACP) Legal Defense Fund against the Office of Civil Rights (OCR) in the U.S. Department of Health, Education and Welfare (HEW) for failing to take action against states that were purportedly operating dual, segregated systems of higher education. Most, but not all, of these states were in the southeastern part of the country where racial segregation was the law until the 1960s. The suit, which has come to be known as the Adams case because it was filed on behalf of Kenneth Adams, contended that the colleges built for African-Americans in the affected states were being use exclusively by them, while white students were enrolling in the traditionally white institutions, and that a parallel situation held true regarding employment for African-American and white faculty, thus effectively maintaining racial segregation.

In 1973, Judge John Pratt ordered OCR to start proceedings to cut off funds to states that fail to develop acceptable plans for desegregation of their higher education systems. In effect, Judge Pratt required HEW to develop specific affirmative action guidelines, including proposals for faculty desegregation. Eighteen states are now involved in the suit, which is still in varying degrees of resolution. The Department of Education released a report, under threat of subpeona, on 10 of the states in April of 1987, but failed to include an evaluation of the efforts the states have made or to say which states have succeeded in desegregating their colleges or making a good faith effort to do so.

In October 1987, the U.S. Court of Appeals held that the Justice Department had failed to prove that public colleges and universities in Alabama, which is one of the states involved in the Adams case, were segregated because the department had argued that the entire state system was segregated, instead of offering evidence that specific programs receiving federal money had violated the anti-bias laws. This ruling was believed to have adverse implications for the other states as well, even though the faculties at the institutions involved, as in other states across the nation, remain almost entirely white.

Judge Pratt's dismissal of the Adams case in late 1987 appears to terminate the involvement of the federal government—at least in the states affected by the court decision—as a significant player in efforts to bring about increased representation of African-Americans and Hispanics on the faculties of predominantly white institutions. The reason given for dismissing the case was that the organizations that had initiated the suit no longer had any legal standing to continue it. Pratt acknowledged that the plaintiffs in the case had suffered discrimination, but added that the discrimination must be fairly traceable to government action or inaction, and that the alleged wrong could be addressed by the suit. As a result the case was dismissed, and with it the threat that colleges and universities would have federal funds reduced or eliminated unless they diversified their communities.

An appeal has been filed by the NAACP Legal Defense Fund, so the situation is not concluded at this point. Affirmative action proponents are concerned that without even the threat of economic sanction, institutions will be even more recalcitrant than before in hiring African-American and Hispanic faculty.

One recent court case that may bode well for affirmative action efforts was *Johnson v. Transportation Agency, Santa Clara County, California*. A 6-to-3 Supreme Court decision in April 1987 rejected a reverse discrimination claim, explicitly upheld affirmative action for women for the first time, and approved the kind of voluntary plans that many colleges and universities have, based on hiring goals and availability pools. The court ruled that plans aimed at remedying "manifest imbalances" in the number of women and minority groups employed in traditionally segregated job categories are valid, and that affirmative action may be justified by statistical evidence that fewer minorities are employed than are available, rather than requiring an employer first to admit past discrimination (see *Chronicle of Higher Education* 1987, p. 1). In a manner of speaking, this ruling appears similar to the decision in the Bakke case, but applies to employment rather than to admissions criteria. This case also seems to be consistent with the AAUP position opposing quotas but supporting the affirmative consideration of sex or race in hiring decisions.

A controversial example of court action dealing with affirmative action is the Consent Decree between the University of North Carolina (UNC) System and the U.S. Department of Education. The Consent Decree, a compromise agreement between the parties involved, ended an 11-year dispute between the UNC system and the Office of Civil Rights of the U.S. Department of Education concerning the desegregation of the higher education system in that state. As one of the original states in the Adams case, North Carolina was ordered by Judge Pratt to undertake specific actions to increase the numbers of African-American faculty at the predominantly white public institutions in the state. North Carolina sued the Department of Health, Education and Welfare (from which the Department of Education evolved) in 1979; as a result, the consent decree was developed, effective through December 31, 1988. Because of the suit, the university system reports its progress on affirmative action to the U.S. District Court for the Eastern District of North Carolina in Raleigh, rather than to the OCR officials in Washington. To date, none of the predominantly white campuses in the university system has met its projected goals for increased numbers of African-American faculty.

A recent blow to affirmative action took place just days before President Ronald Reagan left office. The Supreme Court, by a 6-to-3 vote, struck down an ordinance in Richmond, Virginia which guaranteed minorities a greater share of the city's construction contracts. Justice Sandra Day O'Connor, writing for the majority, argued that the city had not specifically proven a level of past discrimination that would justify its 30 percent set-aside rule. The court, for the first time in its ruling on affirmative action cases, stated that it will impose a "strict scrutiny" standard on these types of programs (*Black Issues in Higher Education* 1989, p. 84; *Time* 1989, p. 60).

While that ruling does not specifically address higher education, it is consistent with findings that the legal appeals of individual African-American and Hispanic faculty members are not likely to result in affirmative action success. Analysis of the opinions of federal courts in litigation over faculty employment matters indicates that judicial deference to the academic and professional judgments of faculty and administrators is still the norm (Lee 1985).

Further, African-Americans may be even less successful than other groups: under Title VII of the 1964 Civil Rights Act, 11 African-American faculty members have sued for problems related to alleged tenure discrimination; none has been successful. Yet, of the 34 women who have sued for tenure problems, 18 have won (Burch 1988, p. 7).

Governmental Agencies

Neither advocates nor opponents of affirmative action were encouraged about the impact of the federal government during the Reagan presidency. Advocates resented the administration's initial posture regarding Bob Jones University, wherein it was argued there was no legal ground for denying the university a tax exemption despite its ban on interracial

dating and marriage. On the other hand, conservatives, such as Terry Eastland, formerly with the Justice Department, were disappointed because

> *the Administration not only had the opportunity to reconcile government programs with the principle of nondiscrimination, but also had the chance to go beyond legal discussions and to encourage constructive debate on how to achieve equal opportunity* (Chronicle of Higher Education 1988, p. A16).

Within the federal government, the Office of Civil Rights (OCR) is the federal agency most directly involved with affirmative action enforcement in higher education. Among its responsibilities are conducting compliance reviews, negotiating corrective actions, investigating individual complaints of discrimination, and preparing legal sanctions when necessary. The Higher Education Division within the OCR operates regional branches which initiate and follow up on compliance reviews, conduct complaint investigations, seek voluntary compliance through negotiations, provide institutions of higher education with technical assistance in all areas related to their equal opportunity programs, and maintain liaison with concerned civil rights groups and organizations (*Education* 1975, pp. 209–10).

In particularly difficult or protracted affirmative action disputes, the Justice Department may also become involved as a monitor. For example, in states that have been accused of operating dual systems of higher education, the Department of Education is currently evaluating desegregation plans that have expired in Arkansas, Delaware, Florida, Georgia, Kentucky, Missouri (involving three universities), North Carolina (involving only the community colleges), Oklahoma, South Carolina, Virginia, and West Virginia (involving one university). The states of Maryland, Pennsylvania, and Texas have had desegregation plans approved by the Department of Education which have not yet expired. The Justice Department has taken over the monitoring of desegregation efforts in Alabama, Louisiana, Mississippi, and Ohio.

Other agencies also might be involved in affirmative action issues, depending on the nature of the complaint. In addition to OCR, the Equal Employment Opportunity Commission, subunits of the Department of Labor, and the State Fair

Employment Practices Commission may participate in the investigation and possible resolution of an affirmative action complaint.

Public Commissions

Undoubtedly the most significant statement on affirmative action from a commission or body of concerned citizens was the report issued by the Carnegie Council on Policy Studies in Higher Education in 1975 titled, *Making Affirmative Action Work in Higher Education.* Recognizing the importance of affirmative action, the Council members—including college presidents and professors along with officials of education agencies—issued a book-length document that deals with affirmative action from theoretical, practical, and legal perspectives. While acknowledging a clear and urgent need for affirmative action, the council also decried governmental interference into the daily operation of colleges and universities. Optimistically, the council saw higher education as being in "a transition period between actual past deficiencies of major proportions and future achievement of true equality of opportunity." Its report was intended to cover policies and practices during the transition—expected to last five years—until 1980.

On the whole, the report can be seen as a useful document. For example it:

- Offers specific information regarding construction of an affirmative action plan, even identifying the elements of a good plan.
- Explains institutional responsibilities regarding affirmative action.
- Details the role of affirmative action committees.
- Identifies effective recruiting approaches.
- Illustrates salary analyses.
- Clarifies selection procedures and promotion policies from an affirmative action standpoint.

A series of recommendations are provided throughout the text that, if implemented, would assist any institution in increasing its numbers of African-American and Hispanic faculty. These steps are supplemented by specific examples taken by various institutions to increase the effectiveness of their affirmative action efforts.

In July 1987, a task force of the State Higher Education Executive Officers (SHEEO) issued a report on the underrepresentation of minority persons in the predominantly white colleges and universities. The task force examined ways to increase the retention and graduation of African-American students. One way to help achieve this end is by instituting broad-based programs to promote racial and ethnic diversity among higher education's professional ranks (Hollander 1987). This report is important because it was written by a collection of the chief administrators of higher education policy in various states; it is significant that these men and women recognize that at the state level, vigorous involvement, stronger incentives, and more penalties are needed to promote successful affirmative action.

The prospect of a federal cutoff of funds for laxity in affirmative action is a psychological deterrent to an institution. However, the realization that no college or university has ever been penalized in this dramatic fashion encourages institutions that evade affirmative action. Public colleges and universities in particular are extremely dependent on state funds, perhaps more so than on federal monies. As a result, pronouncements from the individuals who coordinate the state mechanisms for funding these colleges and universities are likely to be listened to with great seriousness.

The SHEEO report spells out the importance of recruitment and hiring guidelines, and calls for the monitoring of results at the state, as well as the federal, level. Putting this guideline into practice could have a beneficial effect upon affirmative action, because it puts the oversight at a closer level and opens the possibility for sharing information and coordinated enforcement strategies between state and federal agencies. The commission calls for all state higher education officers to join in this task, which could lead to a far more comprehensive system to promote and facilitate greater African-American and Hispanic faculty representation.

A major new commission was recently co-sponsored by the Education Commission of the States and the American Council on Education, the nation's largest organization of colleges and universities. In 1988 the new Commission on Minority Participation in Education and American Life issued a report entitled *One-Third of a Nation*. The commission, composed primarily of major business and political figures, seeks to alert the nation to the serious problem of declining African-American and Hispanic participation in all aspects of American life, including higher education. Undoubtedly, the inability of affirmative action to significantly increase the numbers of African-American and Hispanic faculty in predominantly white institutions will be examined by this new commission, and perhaps strategies for adding to those numbers will be provided.

Professional Organizations

In addition to the new commission that it recently formed, ACE already has a Commission on Minorities in Higher Education composed of college presidents from a variety of predominantly African-American and predominantly white higher education institutions and from major education associations. That group regularly reviews and assesses issues related to the presence of nonwhite people in the nation's colleges and universities. With the support of this commission, ACE issues an annual status report on minority presence in education through its Office of Minority Concerns. These reports frequently provide updates of government statistics that are not publicly distributed, showing the rates of employment for African-American and Hispanic faculty in higher education.

The American Association for University Professors (AAUP) has also issued statements supporting the implementation of affirmative action practices. AAUP has chapters that represent faculty interests and concerns at a number of college and university campuses throughout the nation. In its official publication, *Academe*, the association regularly publishes figures that illustrate the proportional rate of employment of faculty by race and gender.

Various professional associations that represent various academic disciplines, such as the American Sociological Association, the American Psychological Association, and the American Historical Association have endorsed the need for affirmative action to increase racial diversity among the faculty ranks. Despite the statements of support from these and other avenues, the actual effect of affirmative action, in terms of increased numbers of African-American and Hispanic faculty, has been negligible.

CONCLUSIONS AND RECOMMENDATIONS

Access to higher education is primarily a "social process" deeply embedded in the society's cultural patterns and value systems (Thresher 1966). Thus, the relationship between the nation's colleges and the broader society must be kept in mind as this monograph is read (see Thomas 1986).

There are few issues in higher education that are as controversial as affirmative action. Colleges and universities in the United States have reflected the same social values that exist in the larger society; as a result, these institutions have been racially segregated for the greater part of the nation's history. Affirmative action—specific efforts to increase the representation of groups that had been excluded from the mainstream of society—was mandated by the federal government as a means of correcting the effects of prior discrimination. Yet, these programs, by and large, have been extraordinarily ineffective in increasing the representation of African-American and Hispanic faculty at predominantly white colleges and universities. White women, however, have made some gains in the faculty ranks as a result of affirmative action.

The key variable is the attitudes and perspectives of those faculty members who already hold positions in the department or programs where the vacancy exists.

This monograph demonstrates that a combination of individual, institutional, and societal racism explains the absence of African-American and Hispanic faculty in predominantly white colleges and universities. The authors have reviewed many factors which contribute to this situation: changes in educational policy, declines in the pool of African-American and Hispanic graduate students, faculty search traditions, and institutional ambiguity in the commitment to affirmative action.

Affirmative action programs have fundamentally failed due to the lack of leadership and commitment by institutional heads, faculty resistance in the name of standards or quality, and because they have been designed with little or no philosophical or conceptual basis in relation to the overriding purpose and mission of educational institutions.

The success, or failure, of affirmative action efforts has also been attributed to the lack of a well-designed plan, weak availability pools, the strength of the affirmative action officer, and the overall commitment of the particular institution.

All of these factors are important to a degree in the hiring of nonacademic personnel, but in terms of hiring faculty, especially African-Americans and Hispanics, the key variable is the attitudes and perspectives of those faculty members who already hold positions in the department or program where the vacancy exists. We are cognizant of Niara Sudar-kasa's warning that "it will be impossible to significantly increase the representation of African-Americans, other minorities, and women in higher education unless we decrease the overrepresentation of white males. And, there's the rub" (Sudarkasa 1987, p. 5).

In the final analysis, the judgment of a policy is whether the desired results have been achieved. Judging affirmative action on the basis of the efforts made by a college or university is tantamount to judging a student's paper or project on the degree of effort that went into producing it, rather than on the actual quality of the finished product.

White males dominate the faculty ranks in the nation's colleges and universities; it is they who determine who will be allowed to join their ranks. Despite affirmative action, the numbers of African-Americans holding faculty positions at predominantly white institutions is actually smaller than it was at the beginning of the 1980s, and the number of Hispanics holding such positions has increased only marginally. In spite of repeated legal attacks, affirmative action has been upheld in the courts as a legal and viable means of responding to a history of segregation and unequal opportunity. Despite the judicial validation, affirmative action in higher education remains elusive and unfulfilled.

The function of colleges and universities goes beyond providing students with the necessary cognitive skills to allow them to pursue their chosen career. The arena of higher education provides an important stage on which the perspectives of many of the next generation of leaders are shaped and developed. It is unwise to allow white students to perpetuate the myth of nonwhite racial inferiority, when this stereotype could be effectively negated through contact with African-American or Hispanic instructors in the classroom. The social benefit of affirmative action is not simply for African-Americans and Hispanics; it is for the whole nation, for the present and for the future as well.

A truly diverse faculty furthers the mission of the university by producing new knowledge that regularly challenges and enriches both traditional research and traditional curricula. Such a faculty has the capacity to make unique contributions as well as to produce new role models and mentors for students, new stimulation in the classroom, and a more nurturing academic atmosphere.

This monograph points to the need for stronger advocacy approaches to affirmative action. Advocacy differs from compliance in that it is proactive and goal-generating rather than reactive and subservient to externally imposed federal guidelines. Advocacy replaces a passive nondiscrimination philosophy with aggressive recruitment and sustained support of faculty once they are hired. Affirmative action advocacy requires a written and detailed statement of affirmative action policy going well beyond the statement that the university is an "AA/EEO employer;" this policy must be tied to the mission of the academic community, disseminated widely and continuously, and emphasized publicly on appropriate occasions by the president and other spokespersons. The goal of advocacy is not a pseudo-attempt to improve numerical representation but a widespread change in attitude (see Ohio State University 1985).

An effective advocacy program also requires full participation by the entire university community. Visible and committed support by campus leaders is essential—so is active participation by administrative units such as the board of trustees and the deans, faculty units such as the university senate and the departments, student units such as admissions and student affairs, and staff organizations.

A window of opportunity *now* exists through which affirmative action can be implemented. One-third or more of the professoriat will probably be replaced by the end of the century. In the process of hiring their successors, many college and university officials would like to remedy the present dearth of minority group members.

Yet, without stronger advocacy, the new generation of professors that will oversee the nation's college classrooms by the year 2000 could be as racially homogeneous as previous generations, even though in some states, *the majority of students they teach will come from minority groups.*

An advocacy program for faculty should aim deliberately at cultivating this diversity in all of the university's academic programs. All academic units should be asked to collaborate with the affirmative action officer in formulating realistic affirmative action objectives, along with strategies for achieving these objectives in the recruitment, retention, and promotion of scientists, scholars, and teachers from all the targeted groups. Units should then be held responsible for achieving these objectives.

A substantial increase in the number of minority professionals is essential to achieve equity for African-Americans and Hispanics in higher education and in the society at large. The rate of change in the racial composition of doctoral recipients is so slow as to be socially insignificant. Racial parity cannot be achieved even within 100 years, assuming the rate of doctorates awarded to African-Americans and Hispanics remains the same.

The African-American professoriat recognizes a void in the representation of African-American faculty concerns. About 175 African-American faculty attended the inaugural conference of the National Congress of Black Faculty on October 23–25, 1987, which focused on several areas of concern to African-American faculty including hiring, promotion and tenure, research funding and publication, and government relations. The importance of mentoring relationships for African-American students was also stressed *(Black Issues in Higher Education* 1987, pp. 1, 11, 13; *Higher Education and National Affairs* 1987, p. 2).

The mentoring of African-American graduate students has been accomplished most successfully, but not exclusively, by African-American faculty (Blackwell 1987). This finding is not surprising, given that African-American faculty members have both a direct knowledge of the processes and procedures that must be addressed in order to move successfully through graduate school, as well as a sensitivity to cultural nuances that may be manifested by African-American students. One would imagine that the same situation exists with Hispanic graduate students and Hispanic faculty members. Still, the realization that the overwhelming majority of faculty are white makes it necessary that they are also willing and prepared to mentor minority graduate students, just as they now mentor white students. Affirmative action would be best served by simultaneously increasing the numbers of African-American and Hispanic faculty and by having more willing white faculty increase their mentoring activities with minority students.

This monograph concludes by offering action strategies and recommendations in three areas: public policy, higher education practice, and research needs.

Public Policy

If affirmative action in higher education is to result in increased representation of African-Americans and Hispanics in predominantly white colleges and universities, the Bush administration must instruct the Office of Civil Rights to withhold federal funds from institutions that have most conspicuously failed to hire faculty from these underrepresented groups. Only by taking this action, which in fact upholds the law of the land, will colleges and universities move toward actually implementing affirmation action.

Similar sanctions should be put into place at the state level for all institutions of higher education that receive state support. Based on the representation of nonwhite people within the state, colleges and universities should be required to show increased hiring of persons from the underrepresented groups on their faculties, or suffer reductions in the level of funding that they receive from the state treasury. As at the federal level, the determinant of success must be based on results, not simply effort.

Federal and state policy can also have a decisive impact on the supply of African-American and Hispanic faculty members. Both the federal and state governments should play a more aggressive role in the financial support of African-American and Hispanic scholars in both doctoral and undergraduate study.

Higher Education Practices

An incentive program to reward affirmative action would be more effective than added regulations. At a time when resources for higher education have become unpleasantly scarce, monetary incentives would probably have a significant effect. Further, an incentive system would reward voluntary change, rather than impose externally regulated change; for this reason an incentive system is likely to meet with less resistance (Loeb, Ferber, and Lowry 1978).

For many institutions, the effort to entice departments or programs to hire more African-American and Hispanic faculty has been based on an appeal to common decency or on the prospect of a reward, such as an additional faculty position for the unit involved. Along with this carrot, administrative officials also need to use a stick: the reduction or removal of departmental resources from those units that refuse to implement affirmative action. As an example of a penalty, travel or secretarial support to uncooperative departments could be reduced to convey the importance of affirmative action as an institutional priority. Continued intransigence should lead to loss of a faculty position.

With affirmative action advocacy, results rather than procedures should be emphasized, and incentives should be provided by the federal and state governments, as well as by academic communities, for demonstrated improvement in affirmative action hiring and staff treatment. Procedural compliance clearly does not guarantee results. Thus, it seems reasonable to redesign affirmative action programs in order to build incentives geared directly toward the results desired: equity in hiring, pay, and rank.

Institutions of higher education must also look beyond their immediate hiring needs in efforts to contribute to the development of the pool of potential African-American and Hispanic faculty. In the report, *Target Date 2000 AD: Goals for Achieving Higher Education Equity for Black Americans*, the National Advisory Committee on Black Higher Education and Black Colleges and Universities (1980b) urge colleges to improve in five areas. The list includes increasing the number of minority faculty and administrators; the pool of minorities prepared to enroll in higher education; the number of minorities enrolled in higher education, especially in degree programs and scientific and technical fields; the opportunities for minorities to enroll in graduate and professional schools; and the retention and graduation rate of minorities at all levels of education. This monograph illustrates many examples of colleges and universities that are providing leadership in these areas.

Colleges and universities can also address minority faculty needs by seeking candidates for faculty positions outside the traditional ranks of new Ph.D.s. Corporations, the military, industry, and government are a potentially rich source of minority faculty. Also, other innovative approaches, such as faculty exchanges with African-American institutions or visiting appointments, should be expanded. Hiring African-American or Hispanic instructors who have not quite finished their dissertations—if they are provided appropriate support—gives them a foot in the door (Green 1989).

Research Needs
Additional research is needed on the dynamics of faculty search committees, since these are the initial avenues through which African-Americans and Hispanics either gain or are denied faculty positions. By the same token, studies of tenure-

granting committees should be undertaken to further determine when and how such bodies review nonwhites differently from white candidates.

Since the proportion of African-Americans and Hispanics who hold faculty positions in predominantly white colleges and universities does not equal the number of persons from these groups who receive doctorates, it is also important to find where these potential faculty members are, and to determine what it would take to entice them into academe.

Other research needs are the study of the comparative working conditions and career development of African-American, Hispanic, and white faculty; the specific status and needs of African-American and Hispanic women; and factors contributing to the successful retention and promotion of African-American and Hispanic faculty.

Final Comments

Affirmative Rhetoric, Negative Action characterizes the impact of affirmative action on African-American and Hispanic faculty at predominantly white, four-year colleges and universities in the United States today. This monograph illustrates that a "succession of exclusions" (Smelsher and Content 1980, p. 26), inherent in all decisions about the hiring and promotion of African-American and Hispanic faculty, works against minorities at every stage of the process.

Racial inequality in academe is likely to persist as long as a regulatory compliance approach is considered sufficient evidence of affirmative action commitment. Proactive advocacy is needed to redress immediately the discriminatory hiring practices and to address the competing interests, value conflicts, and organizational dilemmas that characterize affirmative action in higher education. Stronger, race-conscious government and institutional action is needed if our national commitment to equal educational opportunity is to be honored.

As Harvard President Derek Bok observed, colleges and universities "did not provide adequate opportunities for women and minorities until (they were) required to do so" and "will not necessarily meet their obligations to society if they are left entirely to their own devices" (Bok 1975, p. 4).

REFERENCES

The Educational Resources Information Center (ERIC) Clearinghouse
on Higher Education abstracts and indexes the current literature
on higher education for inclusion in ERIC's data base and announce-
ment in ERIC's monthly bibliographic journal, *Resources in Education* (RIE). Most of these publications are available through the
ERIC Document Reproduction Service (EDRS). For publications
cited in this bibliography that are available from EDRS, ordering
number and price code are included. Readers who wish to order
a publication should write to the ERIC Document Reproduction
Service, 3900 Wheeler Avenue, Alexandria, Virginia 22304. (Phone
orders with VISA or MasterCard are taken at 800/227-ERIC or 703/
823-0500.) When ordering, please specify the document (ED) number. Documents are available as noted in microfiche (MF) and paper
copy (PC). If you have the price code ready when you call EDRS,
an exact price can be quoted. The last page of the latest issue of
Resources in Education also has the current cost, listed by code.

Abel, Emily. 1981. "Collective Protest and the Meritocracy: Faculty
    Women and Sex Discrimination Lawsuits." *Feminist Studies* 7:
    508.

Allen, Walter R. May/June 1987. "Black Colleges vs. White Colleges.
    The Fork in the Road for Black Students." *Change*: 28–34.

American Association of University Professors. 1982. "Recommended
    Procedures for Increasing the Number of Minority Persons and
    Women on College and University Faculties." *Academe* 68: 15A–
    20A.

American Council on Education. 1987. "Background Paper I: A Status
    Report on Minorities in Higher Education." Washington, D.C.

Andrulis, Dennis P. 1975. "Black Professionals in Predominantly
    White Institutions of Higher Education—An Examination of Some
    Demographic and Mobility Characteristics." *Journal of Negro Edu-
    cation* 44(1): 6–11.

Arbeiter, Solomon. May/June 1987. "Black Enrollments. The Case
    of the Missing Students." *Change*: 14–19.

Arciniega, T. (chair). June 1985. *Hispanics and Higher Education:
    A CSU Imperative*. Final Report of the Commission on Hispanic
    Underrepresentation. Long Beach, Calif.: Office of the Chancellor,
    California State University.

Arkansas State Department of Higher Education. October 1984.
    "Quality Development in Higher Education to Meet the Future
    Needs of Arkansas." Report of the Quality Higher Education Study
    Committee. Little Rock, Ark.: Author. ED 268 859. MF–01;
    PC–04.

Bayer, Alan E. 1972a. *The Black College Freshman: Characteristics
    and Recent Trends*. Washington, D.C.: American Council on
    Education.

————. 1972b. *Teaching Faculty in Academe.* Washington, D.C.: American Council on Education.

Bell, Derrick. 1982. "Preferential Affirmative Action." *Harvard Civil Rights–Civil Liberties Law Review* 16(3): 855–73.

Benokraitis, Nina, and Feagin, Joe. 1978. *Affirmative Action and Equal Opportunity.* Boulder, Colo.: Westview Press.

Bishop, David. 1983. "The Consent Decree between the University of North Carolina System and the U.S. Department of Education, 1981–1982." *Journal of Negro Education* 52(3): 350–61.

Black, Albert, Jr. 1981. "Affirmative Action and the Black Academic Situation." *Western Journal of Black Studies* 5(2): 87–94.

Black Issues in Higher Education. 1 September 1985a: 3.

————. 1 December 1985b: 2.

————. 15 June 1986a.

————. 1 October 1986b: 6.

————. 1 March 1987a: 12.

————. 1 April 1987b: 1–5.

————. 15 May 1987c: 3.

————. 15 August 1987d: 1, 8.

————. 1 October 1987e: 5.

————. 1 November 1987f: 1, 6, 8–10, 17.

————. 15 November 1987g: 1, 11, 13.

————. 1 March 1988a: 6–8.

————. 1 March 1988b, Special Issue on Faculty.

————. 15 July 1988c: 9.

————. 15 September 1988d: 19.

————. 29 September 1988e: 8.

————. 2 March 1989: 84.

Blackwell, James E. 1981. *Mainstreaming Outsiders: The Production of Black Professionals.* 2d rev. ed. New York: General Hall.

————. 1983. "Strategies for Improving the Status of Blacks in Higher Education." *Planning and Changing* 14(1): 56–73.

————. 21 November 1987. "Faculty Roles in Mentoring Minority Students." Paper presented at the Conference on the Role of Faculty in Meeting the National Need for African-American, American Indian, and Latino Scholars at the Harrison Conference Center, Glen Cove, N.Y.

Blake, Elias. May/June 1987. "Equality for Blacks: Another Lost Decade or New Surge Forward?" *Change:* 10–13.

Bloom, Allan. 1987. *The Closing of the American Mind.* New York: Simon and Schuster.

Bok, Derek C. 1975. "Harvard: Then, Now and the Future." *Harvard Today* 18(3): 4.

Bowen, Howard, and Schuster, Jack. 1986. *A National Resource Imperiled.* New York: Oxford University Press.

Boyd, William. 1988. "Creative Strategies for Minority Faculty Recruitment." Paper presented at the Minority Faculty Development Conference, Robert Wood Johnson Medical School, April 29, Piscataway, N.J.

Brown, Shirley Vining. 1988. *Increasing Minority Faculty: An Elusive Goal.* Princeton, N.J.: Educational Testing Service.

Burch, Sallie. 1 March 1988. "Climbing the Professional Ladder: Black Faculty Face Persistent Challenges." *Black Issues in Higher Education*: 1.

Calmore, John. 1986. "National Housing Policies and Black America: Trends, Issues, and Implications." In *The State of Black America*, edited by James Williams. New York: National Urban League.

Cameron, Susan, and Blackburn, Robert. July/August 1981. "Sponsorship and Academic Career Success." *Journal of Higher Education* 52(4): 369–77.

Carnegie Council on Policy Studies in Higher Education. 1975. *Making Affirmative Action Work in Higher Education.* San Francisco: Jossey-Bass.

Carnegie Foundation for the Advancement of Teaching. May/June 1987. "Minority Access: A Question of Equity." *Change*: 35–39.

Carter, George E. April 1981. "Affirmative Action in Higher Education: Another Political Myth for Ethnic Americans." Paper presented at the Annual Regional Southwest Pacific Conference of the National Association of Interdisciplinary Ethnic Studies and the Annual Conference on Ethnic Minority Studies of the National Association of Interdisciplinary Ethnic Studies. Santa Clara, Calif. ED 217 114. 17 pp. MF–01; PC–01.

Cartwright, Carol. 15 August 1987. "Interview." *Black Issues in Higher Education* (11)4: 1–2.

Census Bureau. 1973, 1978, 1980, 1984. "Population Characteristics: Social and Economic Characteristics of Students." Current Population Reports. Washington, D.C.: Government Printing Office.

Census Bureau. 1980. *1980 Census of Population.* Vol. I, Ch. B, Pt. 37. PC 80–1–B–37. Washington, D.C.: Government Printing Office.

Census Bureau. 1987. *Educational Attainment in the United States.* March 1982 to 1985. Washington, D.C.: Government Printing Office.

Change. May/June 1987.

Children's Defense Fund. 1989. *A Vision of America's Future.* Washington, D.C.: CDF.

Chronicle of Higher Education. 10 September 1986; 1, 24.

———. 1 April 1987a: 1.

———. 10 September 1987b: 24.

———. 30 September 1987c: 1.

———. 29 June 1988: A14, A16, A17.

The Commission on Minority Participation in Education and American Life. May 1988. *One-Third of a Nation: An American Imperative.* Washington, D.C.: American Council on Education, Education Commission of the States.

Coughlin, Patrick J. 1986. "Mainstreaming Affirmative Action—A Practitioner Speaks." *Journal of the College and University Personnel Association* 37(4): 27–28.

Dennis, Rodney, and Silver, Joseph. 1988. "Factors Related to Hiring and Career Advancement of Black Faculty on Traditionally White Campuses." Report presented at the American Association on Higher Education National Conference, March 10, Washington, D.C.

Dingerson, M. R.; Rodman, J. A.; and Wade, J. F. 1982. "Procedures and Costs for Hiring Academic Administrators." *Journal of Higher Education* 53: 63–74.

Dunran, R. P. 1983. Hispanics' Education and Background—Predictors of College Achievement. New York: College Entrance Examination Board.

Dziech, B. W., and Weiner, L. 1984. *The Lecherous Professor.* New York: Beacon Press.

Eastland, Terry, and Bennett, William. 1979. *Counting by Race.* New York: Basic Books.

Ebony. October 1947: 16.

Education. 1975: 209–10.

Educational Record. Winter 1988: 17, 19.

Elmore, C., and Blackburn, Robert T. 1983. "Black and White Faculty in White Research Universities." *Journal of Higher Education* 54(1): 1–15.

Escobedo, Theresa. October 1980. "Are Hispanic Women in Higher Education the Non-Existent Minority?" *Educational Researcher* 9(9): 7–12.

Exum, William. 1983. "Climbing the Crystal Stair: Values, Affirmative Action and Minority Faculty." *Social Problems* 30(4): 383–99.

Feldman, Saul D. 1974. *Escape from the Doll's House, Carnegie Commission on Higher Education.* New York: McGraw-Hill.

Fendley, William R., Jr., and others. October 1979. "A Methodology to Study Promotion, Tenure and Termination Among Academic Faculty at the University of Tennessee, Knoxville." Paper presented at the Annual Meeting of the Southern Association for Institutional Research, Orlando, Fla. ED 180 368. 17 pp. MF–01; PC–01.

Fields, Cheryl. 16 September 1987. "Closing the Gap for Hispanics: State Aims to Forestall a Divided Society." *Chronicle of Higher Education*: 1.

————. 6 January 1988a. "Judge Dismisses the Case for 15 Years to Prod States, U.S. on Campus Segregation." *Chronicle of Higher Education*: 1.

————. 11 May 1988b. "Hispanics, State's Fastest-Growing Minority, Shut Out of Top Positions at University of California, Leaders Say." *Chronicle of Higher Education*: 9–10.

Finkelstein, Martin J. 1982. "Women and Minority Faculty: A Synthesis of Extant Empirical Researchers." *Resources in Education.* ED 219 015. 73 pp. MF–01; PC–03.

————. 1983. *The American Academic Profession: A Synthesis of Social Scientific Inquiry since World War II.* Columbus, Ohio: OSU Press.

Finn, Chester E., Jr. 1982. "Affirmative Action Under Reagan." *Commentary* 73: 17–22.

Fiske, E. B. 28 November 1982. "Fewer Blacks Enter Universities: Recession and Aid Cuts Are Cited." *New York Times*: 1+.

Fleming, John E.; Gill, Gerald R.; and Swinton, David H. 1978. *The Case for Affirmative Action for Blacks in Higher Education.* Institute for the Study of Educational Policy. Washington, D.C.: Howard University Press.

Florida State Department of Education. September 1974. "Report of the Florida Public Community College Equal Access/Equal Opportunity Consulting Team." Tallahassee: Author. ED 116 722. 205 pp. MF–01; PC–09.

Ford Foundation. 1969. *A Survey of Black American Doctorates: A Report.* New York: Author.

Fortunata, Ray T. 1985. "Affirmative Action and Personnel Administration Functions: A Case for Alliance." *Journal of the College and University Personnel Association* 36: 46–50.

Franklin, Stephen. 1 October 1988. "Lack of Progress in Hiring Black Faculty Continues to Vex Higher Education," *Black Issues in Higher Education*: 1.

Galambos, Eva. 1979. *Racial Composition of Faculties in Public Colleges and Universities of the South.* Atlanta, Ga.: Southern Regional Education Board.

Garza, Hisauro. Winter 1988. "The 'Barrioization' of Hispanic Faculty." *Educational Record*: 122–24.

Goodwin, James C. 1975. "Playing Games with Affirmative Action." *Chronicle of Higher Education* 10: 24.

Gray, Mary W., and Schafer, Alice T. December 1981. "Guidelines for Equality: A Proposal." *Academe* 67: 351–54.

Green, Madeline. 1989. *Minorities on Campus: A Handbook for Enhancing Diversity.* Washington, D.C.: American Council on Education.

Hale, Frank W., Jr. 1975. "A Sprinkle of Pepper: The State of Black Influence in White Colleges and Universities." *Journal of Non-White Concerns in Personnel and Guidance* 3(2): 45–52.

Hall, M. L., and Allen, W. R. January/April 1982. "Race Consciousness and Achievement: Two Issues in the Study of Black Graduate/

Professional Studies." *Integrateducation* 20: 56–61.

Hankin, Joseph N. June 1984a. "Affirmative Action in Two-Year Colleges, 1983–1984." Paper presented at the Annual National Conference on Issues Facing Black Administrators at Predominantly White Colleges and Universities. June, Cambridge, Mass. ED 244 710. 10 pp. MF–01; PC–01.

———. 1984b. "Where the (Affirmative) Action Is: The Status of Minorities and Women among the Faculty and Administrators of Public Two-Year Colleges, 1983–1984." *Journal of the College and University Personnel Association* 35(4): 36–39.

———. November 1986. *Affirmative Action and Inaction: The Status of Minorities and Women at Public Two-Year Colleges in New York State and the Nation.* Albany, N.Y.: State of University of New York, Nelson A. Rockefeller Institute of Government. ED 279 380. 14 pp. MF–01; PC–01.

Harvey, William B. 30 September 1981. "Racism on Campus: College Must Take Positive Steps to Eradicate the Disease." *Chronicle of Higher Education*: 56.

———. 1985. "Excellence and Cultural Pluralism." *Teacher Education and Practice* 2: 47–50.

———. 22 January 1986. "Where Are the Black Faculty: In the Lingering Climate of Institutional Racism, They Are Not the Only Losers." *Chronicle of Higher Education* 96.

———. 23 November 1987. "Much Pain and No Gain: An Update on Black Faculty Representation in Higher Education." Paper presented at the Annual Meeting of the Association for the Study of Higher Education.

———. 1988a. "Fostering Minority Faculty Retention through the Campus Environment." Paper presented at the Minority Faculty Development Conference, Robert Wood Johnson Medical School, April 29, Piscataway, N.J.

———. 1988b. "The State of the Profession: Faculty Concerns and Considerations." In *Points of View: Issues in American Higher Education*, edited by S. Barnes. Lewiston, N.Y.: Edwin Mellen Press.

Harvey, William B., and Scott-Jones, Diane. 1985. "We Can't Find Any: The Elusiveness of Black Faculty Members in American Higher Education." *Issues in Education* 3(1): 68–76.

Hayward, Gerald C., and Barbarita, Juana. January 1981. Report to the State Legislature on the Progress of the California Community Colleges Affirmative Action Program. Sacramento, Calif.: California Community Colleges, Office of the Chancellor. ED 200 259. 109 pp. MF–01; PC–05.

Henry, Samuel D. September/October 1985. "Affirmative Action in Higher Education: Toward a Theory of the Desegregation of the Workplace." *The Black Scholar*: 23–30.

Higgerson, Mary Lou, and Higgerson, Richard. 1 July 1987. "The

Supreme Court's Decision on Affirmative Action: Progress and Pitfalls." *Chronicle of Higher Education*: 68.

Higgerson, Mary Lou, and Hinchcliff-Pias, Mary. Fall 1982. "Affirmative Action: A Time to Reverse Our Approach." *Journal of College and University Personnel Association* 33: 26–35.

Higher Education and National Affairs. 16 November 1987: 2, 3.

————. 1 February 1988: 5.

————. 6 June 1988: 5.

————. 4 July 1988.

Higher Education Fact Sheet No. 11. May 1982. Department of Education, National Advisory Committee on Black Higher Education and Black Colleges and Universities.

Hill, Richard J. 1983. "Minorities, Women, and Institutional Change: Some Administrative Concerns." *Sociological Perspectives* 26(1): 17–28.

Hirsch, E. D. 1987. *Cultural Literacy: What Every American Should Know*. New York: Houghton Mifflin.

Hodgkinson, Harold. 1985. *All One System*. Washington, D.C.: Institute for Educational Leadership.

Hollander, T. E. 1987. *A Difference of Degrees: State Initiatives to Improve Minority Student Achievement*. Denver, Colo.: State Higher Education Executive Offices.

Hornig, Lilli S. September 1979. "Untenured and Tenuous: The Status of Women Faculty in Academe." TS submitted for publication to *The Annals of the American Academy of Political and Social Science* 16.

Hyer, Patricia. 1985. "Affirmative Action for Women Faculty: Case Study of Three Successful Institutions." *Journal of Higher Education* 56: 282–99.

Institute for the Study of Educational Policy. 1978. *Affirmative Action for Blacks in Higher Education: A Report*. Washington, D.C.: Author.

Jacques, Jeffrey M., and Hall, Robert L. 1980. Integration of the Black and White University: A Preliminary Investigation. Tallahassee: Florida Research Center. ED 212 177. 160 pp. MF–01; PC–07.

Jaschik, Scott. 8 April 1987a. "Education Department Reports on Desegregation but Includes No Evaluation of State Efforts." *Chronicle of Higher Education*: 18.

————. 6 May 1987b. "Recruiting Plans Found Lacking at Many Colleges Where Desegregation Plans Have Expired." *Chronicle of Higher Education*: 19.

Jensen, A. R. 1969. "How Much Can We Boost IQ and Scholastic Achievement?" *Harvard Educational Review* 39: 1–123.

Jordan, Vernon E. 1979. "How Far We Still Must Go." *AGB Reports* 21(4): 10–14.

Kentucky Commission on Human Rights. October 1982. *Number and Percent of Black Faculty at State Universities Decline from 1979 to 1981*. Staff Report 82–10. Louisville, Ky.: Author. ED 237 608. 38 pp. MF–01; PC–02.

Koch, J. V., and Chizmar, J. F., Jr. March 1976. "Sex Discrimination and Affirmative Action in Faculty Salaries." *Economic Inquiry*. 16–23.

Lambert, Linda, and others. 1980. *Target 2000 AD: Goals for Achieving Higher Education Equity for Black Americans, Volume I*. Washington, D.C.: National Advisory Committee on Black Higher Education and Black Colleges and Universities.

Lee, Barbara. 1985. "Federal Court Involvement in Academic Personnel Decisions: Impact on Peer Review." *Journal of Higher Education* 56: 38–54.

Lester, R. A. 1974. "Antibias Regulation of Universities: Faculty Problems and their Solutions." A report prepared for the Carnegie Commission on Higher Education. New York: McGraw-Hill.

Lewin, A. Y., and Duchan, L. "Women in Academia." *Science* 176: 34–35.

Loeb, J. W.; Ferber, M. A.; and Lowry, H. M. 1978. "The Effectiveness of Affirmative Action for Women." *Journal of Higher Education* 49: 218–30.

Loftus, Elizabeth. January 1977. "Policies of Affirmative Action." *Society* 14.

Maguire, Daniel C. 1980. *A New American Justice: Ending the White Male Monopolies*. New York: Doubleday.

Marable, Manning. 1983. *How Capitalism Underdevelops Black America*. Boston: South End Press.

Marcus, Lawrence C. 1977. "Affirmative Action in Higher Education." *Journal of Intergroup Relations* 6(1): 24–53.

Maryland State Board for Higher Education. December 1980. *A Plan to Assure Equal Postsecondary Educational Opportunity, 1980–1985*. Annapolis, Md.: Author. ED 206 216. 123 pp. MF–01; PC–05.

Massey, Walter. 15 July 1987. "If We Want Racially Tolerant Students, We Must Have More Minority Professors." *Chronicle of Higher Education*: 76.

Menges, Robert J., and Exum, William H. 1983. "Barriers to the Progress of Women and Minority Faculty." *Journal of Higher Education* 54(2): 123–44.

Merriam, Sharan. Spring 1983. "Mentors and Proteges: A Critical Review of the Literature." *Adult Education Quarterly* 33(33): 161–73.

Mingle, James R. 1987a. *Focus on Minorities: Trends in Higher Education Participation and Success*. Denver, Colo.: Education Commission of the States.

————. 1987b. *Focus on Minorities: Synopsis of State Higher Education Initiatives.* Denver, Colo.: Education Commission of the States.

Moore, William, Jr., and Wagstaff, L. H. 1974. *Black Educators in White Colleges.* San Francisco: Jossey-Bass.

Murray, C. December 1984. "Affirmative Racism." *The New Republic:* 18–23.

National Academy of Sciences. 1987. *Nurturing Science and Engineering Talent.* Washington, D.C.: National Academy of Sciences.

National Advisory Committee on Black Higher Education and Black Colleges and Universities. 1980a. *A Losing Battle: The Decline in Black Participation in Graduate and Professional Education.* Washington, D.C.: U.S. Department of Education.

————. 1980b. *Target Date 2000: Goals for Achieving Higher Education Equity for Black Americans. Volume 1.* Washington, D.C.: U.S. Department of Education.

National Center for Educational Statistics. 1985. *The Traditionally Black Institutions of Higher Education, 1960–1982.* Washington, D.C.: NCES, 132 pp.

National Research Council. 1978. *A Century of Doctorates.* Washington, D.C.: National Academy of Sciences.

National Science Foundation. 1988. *Legacy to Tomorrow.* Washington, D.C.: NSF.

National Urban League, Inc. May 1982. *Tri-State Minority Faculty Employment Opportunity Project. Final Report.* New York: Author. ED 236 261. 408 pp. MF–01; PC–17.

New Jersey State Department of Higher Education. April 1983. *Affirmative Action Status Report: 1982–83. New Hires at New Jersey Public Colleges and Universities: Special Report Series.* Trenton, N.J.: Author. ED 233 633. 64 pp. MF–01; PC–03.

Newsweek on Campus. February 1987: 16.

O'Brien, Eileen M. 1 November 1987. "National Organization Created to Represent Black Faculty Concerns and Interests." *Black Issues in Higher Education:* 1.

The Ohio State University. June 1985. *Affirmative Action Advocacy at the Ohio State University. A Report by the President's Committee on Affirmative Action.* Columbus, Ohio: OSU.

Olivas, Michael. 1986. *Latino College Students.* New York: Teachers College Press.

————. May/June 1988. "Latino Faculty at the Border: Increasing Numbers Key to More Hispanic Access." *Change:* 6–9.

Oliver, M. L., and Glick, M. A. 1982. "An Analysis of the New Orthodoxy on Black Mobility." *Social Problems* 29: 511–23.

O'Neil, Robert M. 1973. *Discriminating against Discrimination: Preferential Admissions and the DeFunis Case.* Bloomington, Ind.: Indiana University Press.

————. 1975. "The Colleges and the Courts: A Peacetime Perspective." *Liberal Education* 59: 176–86.

Preer, Jean. 1981. *Minority Access to Higher Education*. ASHE-ERIC Higher Education Research Report No. 1. Washington, D.C.: Association for the Study of Higher Education. ED 207 474.

Pruitt, Anne S. March 1982. "Black Employees in Traditionally White Institutions in the 'Adams' States, 1975 to 1977." Paper presented at the Annual Meeting of the American Education Research Association, New York. ED 215 646. 112 pp. MF–01; PC–03.

Rafky, David M. 1972. *Race Relations in Higher Education*. Syracuse, N.Y.: Syracuse University.

————. February 1973. "Ambiguities in Race Relations: Blacks and Whites in Higher Education." Paper presented at the meeting of the American Educational Research Association. ED 074 924. 34 pp. MF–01; PC–02.

Reed, Rodney, J. 1983. "Affirmative Action in Higher Education: Is It Necessary?" *Journal of Negro Education* 52(3): 322–49.

Rex, Sara. 1987. *The American Woman: 1987–88*. Washington, D.C.: Women's Research and Education Institute.

Romero, Dan. 1977. "The Impact and Use of Minority Faculty within a University." Paper presented at the Annual Meeting of the American Psychological Association, August, San Francisco, Calif. ED 146 240. 23 pp. MF–01; PC–01.

Richardson, Richard C.; Simmons, Howard; and Delos Santos, Alfredo G., Jr. May/June 1987. "Graduating Minority Students: Lessons from Ten Success Stories." *Change* 20–27.

Samuels, Frank. 1985. "Closing the Door: The Future of Minorities in Two-Year Institutions." Paper presented at the National Adult Education Conference of the American Association for Adult and Continuing Education, Milwaukee. ED 263 946. 31 pp. MF–01; PC–02.

Scott, Richard R. 1981a. "Black Faculty Productivity and Interpersonal Academic Contacts." *Journal of Negro Education* 50(3): 224–36.

————. 1981b. *A Social Facilitation Model of Black Faculty Productivity*. Washington, D.C.: Social Science Research Council. ED 227 734. 39 pp. MF–01; PC–02.

Seidman, Earl, and others. April 1983. "The Few among the Many: Interviews of Minority Community College Faculty." Paper presented at the Annual Meeting of the American Education Research Association, Montreal. ED 230 251. MF–01; PC–03.

Simmons, Ron. 1982. *Affirmative Action*. Cambridge, Mass.: Schenkman Publishing.

Smelsher, N. J., and Content, R. 1980. *The Changing Academic Market*. Berkeley, Calif.: University of California Press.

Socolow, D. J. 1978. "How Administrators Get their Jobs." *Change* 10: 42–43.

Sowell, Thomas. 1972. *Black Education: Myths and Tragedies.* New York: McKay Publishing Co.

———. Winter 1976. "Affirmative Action Reconsidered." *The Public Interest*: 47–65.

Spratlen, Thaddeus H. 1979. "The Bakke Decision: Implications for Black Educational and Professional Opportunities." *Journal of Negro Education* 48(4): 449–56.

Staples, Brent. 27 April 1986. "The Dwindling Black Presence on Campus." *New York Times Magazine*: 46–52, 62.

Staples, Robert, and Jones, Terry. March/April 1984. "Racial Ideology and Intellectual Racism: Blacks in Academia." *Black Scholar* 15(2): 2–17.

Stetson, Jeffrey. 1984. "The Illusion of Inclusion: Affirmative Inaction in the Eighties—A Practitioner Speaks." *Journal of the College and University Personnel Association* 35(4): 9–15.

Stindt, Julie. February 1987. *Affirmative Action in California Community Colleges.* Sacramento, Calif.: California Community Colleges. ED 277 441. 310 pp. MF–01; PC–03.

Sudarkasa, Niara. February 1987. "Affirmative Action or Affirmative of the Status Quo? Black Faculty and Administrators in Higher Education." *AAHE Bulletin* 39(6): 3–6.

Tennessee Higher Education Commission. May 1975. *Progress Report on Implementation of Desegregation Plans.* Nashville, Tenn.: Author. ED 118 699. 36 pp. MF–01; PC–02.

Texas Association of Chicanos in Higher Education. June 1986. "The Mexican-Americans and Texas Higher Education." A report presented to the Texas Select Commission on Higher Education. Austin, Tex.: Author. ED 271 283. 14 pp. MF–01; PC–01.

Thomas, Gail E. 1986. *The Access and Success of Blacks and Hispanics in U.S. Graduate and Professional Education.* Washington, D.C.: National Academy Press.

Thresher, B. A. 1966. *College Admissions and the Public Interest.* New York: College Entrance Examination Board.

Time. 6 February 1989: 60.

Today's Education. March 1975: 94.

Tomlinson, Louise. 1988. *An Investigation of Administrative Orientations Regarding Issues of Black Faculty Recruitment and Retention.* Athens, Ga.: University of Georgia.

Trent, William, and Copeland, Elaine. 1987. *Effectiveness of State Financial Aid in the Production of Black Doctoral Recipients.* Atlanta, Ga.: Southern Education Foundation.

Tryman, Mfanya Donald. 1986. "Reversing Affirmative Action: A Theoretical Construct." *Journal of Negro Education* 55(2): 185–99.

U.S. Commission on Civil Rights. 1975. *The Federal Civil Rights Enforcement Effort—1974.* Vol. 3, "To Ensure Equal Educational Opportunity." Washington, D.C.: Government Printing Office.

————. November 1981. *Affirmative Action in the 1980's: Disman-
tling the Process of Discrimination*. U.S. Government Clearinghouse Publication No. 70. Washington, D.C.: Government Printing
Office.

U.S. Congress, House. 1975. Committee on Education and Labor.
"Hearings before the Special Subcommittee on Education and
Labor." 93d Congress. Washington, D.C.: Government Printing
Office. Pp. 181–94.

U.S. News and World Report. 14 January 1980: 63.

University System of Georgia. June 1974. *A Plan for the Further Desegregation of the University System of Georgia*. Atlanta, Ga.: Author.
ED 092 091. 244 pp. MF–01; PC–10.

Valverde, Leonard. October 1980. "Development of Ethnic
Researchers and the Education of White Researchers." *Educational
Researcher* 9(9): 16–20.

————. 1987. "The Role of Graduate Faculty in Bringing Democracy
to Graduate Education." Paper presented at the Conference on
the Role of Faculty in Meeting the National Need for African-
American, American Indian, and Latino Scholars at the Harrison
Conference Center, November 21, Glen Cove, N.Y.

————. May/June 1988. "The Missing Element: Hispanics at the
Top in Higher Education." *Change*: 11.

Van Alstyne, C., and Coldren, S. L. June 1976. *The Costs of Imple-
menting Federally Mandated Social Programs at Colleges and
Universities*. Washington, D.C.: American Council on Education.
Policy Analysis Service.

VanderWaerdt, Lois. 1982. *Affirmative Action in Higher Education:
A Sourcebook*. New York: Garland.

Washington, Valora, and LaPoint, Velma. 1988. *Black Children and
American Institutions: An Ecological Review and Resource Guide*.
New York: Garland.

Weinberg, Meyer. 1977. *Minority Students: A Research Appraisal*.
Washington, D.C.: U.S. Department of Health, Education and
Welfare.

Willie, Charles Vert. 1981. *The Ivory and Ebony Towers: Race Relations and Higher Education*. Lexington, Mass.: Lexington Books.

Wilson, Reginald. May–June 1985. "Affirmative Action: The Current
Status." *AGB Reports*: 17–21.

————. February 1987. "Recruitment and Retention of Minority Faculty and Staff." *AAHE Bulletin* 39(6): 11–14.

Wilson, Reginald, and Melendez, Sarah. 1983, 1984, 1985, 1986, 1987.
Annual Status Report: Minorities in Higher Education. Washington,
D.C.: American Council on Education.

Wisenhunt, D. W. 1980. "Confessions of a Job Seeker or What Price
Compliance?" *Educational Horizons* 58: 109–12.

INDEX

A

National Advisory Committee on Black Higher Education and Black Colleges and Universities, 80
National Aeronautics and Space Administration (NASA), 56
National Association for the Advancement of Colored People (NAACP), 66, 68
National Center for Education Statistics (NCES), 18
National Congress of Black Faculty, 78
National Consortium for Educational Access, 54
National Consortium for Graduate Degrees in Engineering (GEM), 54
National Defense Education Act Fellowships, 39
National Latino Faculty Survey, 27
National Research Council, 34, 55, 59
National Science Foundation (NSF), 22, 38, 55
Native Americans
    compensation for land, 2
    doctorate awards, 35
    lack of progress, 25
    stereotyping, 4
NCES (see National Center for Education Statistics)
Network development, 59
New Jersey
    Association of Affirmative Action in Higher Education, 52
    legislation, 55
    Minority Academic Career Program, 55
New York Central College, 5
North Carolina
    consent decree, 68–69
    desegregation plan, 70
NSF (see National Science Foundation)

O

O'Connor, Sandra Day, 69
Oberlin College, 5, 54
OCR (see Office of Civil Rights)
OFCCP (see Office of Federal Contract Compliance Programs)
Office of Civil Rights (OCR), 18, 35, 37, 66, 67, 68, 70, 79
Office of Federal Contract Compliance Programs (OFCCP), 9–10
Office of Minority Concerns (ACE), 73
Ohio: desegregation efforts, 70
Ohio State University, 53, 56
Oklahoma
    desegregation plan, 70
    federal mandate, 35
"Old boy" network, 12, 47
Olivet College, 6
One Third of a Nation, 72
Ostar, Alan W., 38

University of North Carolina
    at Chapel Hill, 59
    system, 68–69
University of Pennsylvania, 5
University of Puerto Rico, 4
University of the District of Columbia, 56
University of Wisconsin-Madison, 58
Upward Bound, 20, 39

Work study funds, 38
Workforce representation, 41
World War II, 2, 7, 38
Wright, Kenneth E., 52

X
Xavier University, 57

Y
Young Scholars Program, 56

Since 1983, the Association for the Study of Higher Education (ASHE) and the Educational Resources Information Center (ERIC) Clearinghouse on Higher Education, a sponsored project of the School of Education and Human Development at The George Washington University, have cosponsored the *ASHE-ERIC Higher Education Report* series. The 1989 series is the eighteenth overall and the first to be published by the School of Education and Human Development at the George Washington University.

Each monograph is the definitive analysis of a tough higher education problem, based on thorough research of pertinent literature and insitutional experiences. Topics are identified by a national survey. Noted practitioners and scholars are then commissioned to write the reports, with experts providing critical reviews of each manuscript before publication.

Eight monographs (10 before 1985) in the ASHE-ERIC Higher Education Report series are published each year and are available on a individual or subscription basis. Subscription to eight issues is $80.00 annually; $60 to members of AAHE, AIR, or AERA; and $50 to ASHE members. All foreign subscribers must include an additional $10 per series year for postage.

Prices for single copies, including book rate postage, are $15.00 regular and $11.25 for members of AERA, AIR, AAHE, and ASHE ($10.00 regular and $7.50 for members for 1985 to 1987 reports, $7.50 regular and $6.00 for members for 1983 and 1984 reports, $6.50 regular and $5.00 for members for reports published before 1982). All foreign orders must include $1.00 per book for foreign postage. Fast United Parcel Service or first class postage is available for $1.00 per book in the U.S. and $2.50 per book outside the U.S. (orders above $50.00 may substitue 5% of the total invoice amount for domestic postage). Make checks payable to ASHE-ERIC. For VISA and MasterCard payments, include card number, expiration date, and signature. Orders under $25 must be prepaid. Bulk discounts are avilable on order of 15 or more reports (not applicable to subscription orders). Order from the Publications Department, ASHE-ERIC Higher Education Reports, The George Washington University, One Dupont Circle, Suite 630, Washington, DC 20036-1183, or phone us at (202) 296-2597. Write for a complete catalog of all available reports.

1989 ASHE-ERIC Higher Education Reports

1. Making Sense of Administrative Leadership: The 'L' Word in Higher Education
   Estela M. Bensimon, Anna Neumann, and Robert Birnbaum

2. Affirmative Rhetoric, Negative Action: African-American and Hispanic Faculty at Predominantly White Institutions
   Valora Washington and William Harvey

1988 ASHE-ERIC Higher Education Reports

1. The Invisible Tapestry: Culture in American Colleges and Universities
   George D. Kuh and Elizabeth J. Whitt

2. Critical Thinking: Theory, Research, Practice, and Possibilities
   Joanne Gainen Kurfiss

3. Developing Academic Programs: The Climate for Innovation
   Daniel T. Seymour

4. Peer Teaching: To Teach is To Learn Twice
   Neal A. Whitman

5. Higher Education and State Governments: Renewed Partnership, Cooperation, or Competition?
   Edward R. Hines

6. Entrepreneurship and Higher Education: Lessons for Colleges, Universities, and Industry
   James S. Fairweather

7. Planning for Microcomputers in Higher Education: Strategies for the Next Generation
   Reynolds Ferrante, John Hayman, Mary Susan Carlson, and Harry Phillips

8. The Challenge for Research in Higher Education: Harmonizing Excellence and Utility
   Alan W. Lindsay and Ruth T. Neumann

1987 ASHE-ERIC Higher Education Reports

1. Incentive Early Retirement Programs for Faculty: Innovative Responses to a Changing Environment
   Jay L. Chronister and Thomas R. Kepple, Jr.

2. Working Effectively with Trustees: Building Cooperative Campus Leadership
   Barbara E. Taylor

3. Formal Recognition of Employer-Sponsored Instruction: Conflict and Collegiality in Postsecondary Education
   Nancy S. Nash and Elizabeth M. Hawthorne

4. Learning Styles: Implications for Improving Educational Practices
   Charles S. Claxton and Patricia H. Murrell

5. Higher Education Leadership: Enhancing Skills through Professional Development Programs
   Sharon A. McDade

6. Higher Education and the Public Trust: Improving Stature in Colleges and Universities
   Richard L. Alfred and Julie Weissman

7. College Student Outcomes Assessment: A Talent Development

Perspective
Maryann Jacobi, Alexander Astin, and Frank Ayala, Jr.

8. Opportunity from Strength: Strategic Planning Clarified with Case Examples
Robert G. Cope

1986 ASHE-ERIC Higher Education Reports

1. Post-tenure Faculty Evaluation: Threat or Opportunity?
Christine M. Licata

2. Blue Ribbon Commissions and Higher Education: Changing Academe from the Outside
Janet R. Johnson and Laurence R. Marcus

3. Responsive Professional Education: Balancing Outcomes and Opportunities
Joan S. Stark, Malcolm A. Lowther, and Bonnie M.K. Hagerty

4. Increasing Students' Learning: A Faculty Guide to Reducing Stress among Students
Neal A. Whitman, David C. Spendlove, and Claire H. Clark

5. Student Financial Aid and Women: Equity Dilemma?
Mary Moran

6. The Master's Degree: Tradition, Diversity, Innovation
Judith S. Glazer

7. The College, the Constitution, and the Consumer Student: Implications for Policy and Practice
Robert M. Hendrickson and Annette Gibbs

8. Selecting College and University Personnel: The Quest and the Question
Richard A. Kaplowitz

1985 ASHE-ERIC Higher Education Reports

1. Flexibility in Academic Staffing: Effective Policies and Practices
Kenneth P. Mortimer, Marque Bagshaw, and Andrew T. Masland

2. Associations in Action: The Washington, D.C. Higher Education Community
Harland G. Bloland

3. And on the Seventh Day: Faculty Consulting and Supplemental Income
Carol M. Boyer and Darrell R. Lewis

4. Faculty Research Performance: Lessons from the Sciences and Social Sciences
John W. Creswell

5. Academic Program Review: Institutional Approaches, Expec-

tations, and Controversies
Clifton F. Conrad and Richard F. Wilson

6. Students in Urban Settings: Achieving the Baccalaureate Degree
Richard C. Richardson, Jr. and Louis W. Bender

7. Serving More Than Students: A Critical Need for College Student Personnel Services
Peter H. Garland

8. Faculty Participation in Decision Making: Necessity or Luxury?
Carol E. Floyd

1984 ASHE-ERIC Higher Education Reports

1. Adult Learning: State Policies and Institutional Practices
K. Patricia Cross and Anne-Marie McCartan

2. Student Stress: Effects and Solutions
Neal A. Whitman, David C. Spendlove, and Claire H. Clark

3. Part-time Faulty: Higher Education at a Crossroads
Judith M. Gappa

4. Sex Discrimination Law in Higher Education: The Lessons of the Past Decade
J. Ralph Lindgren, Patti T. Ota, Perry A. Zirkel, and Nan Van Gieson

5. Faculty Freedoms and Institutional Accountability: Interactions and Conflicts
Steven G. Olswang and Barbara A. Lee

6. The High Technology Connection: Academic/Industrial Cooperation for Economic Growth
Lynn G. Johnson

7. Employee Educational Programs: Implications for Industry and Higher Education
Suzanne W. Morse

8. Academic Libraries: The Changing Knowledge Centers of Colleges and Universities
Barbara B. Moran

9. Futures Research and the Strategic Planning Process: Implications for Higher Education
James L. Morrison, William L. Renfro, and Wayne I. Boucher

10. Faculty Workload: Research, Theory, and Interpretation
Harold E. Yuker

1983 ASHE-ERIC Higher Education Reports

1. The Path to Excellence: Quality Assurance in Higher Education
Laurence R. Marcus, Anita O. Leone, and Edward D. Goldberg

2. Faculty Recruitment, Retention, and Fair Employment:

Obligations and Opportunities
John S. Waggaman

3. Meeting the Challenges: Developing Faculty Careers*
Michael C.T. Brooks and Katherine L. German

4. Raising Academic Standards: A Guide to Learning Improvement
Ruth Talbott Keimig

5. Serving Learners at a Distance: A Guide to Program Practices
Charles E. Feasley

6. Competence, Admissions, and Articulation: Returning to the Basics in Higher Education
Jean L. Preer

7. Public Service in Higher Education: Practices and Priorities
Patricia H. Crosson

8. Academic Employment and Retrenchment: Judicial Review and Administrative Action
Robert M. Hendrickson and Barbara A. Lee

9. Burnout: The New Academic Disease*
Winifred Albizu Melendez and Rafael M. de Guzmán

10. Academic Workplace: New Demands, Heightened Tensions
Ann E. Austin and Zelda F. Gamson

*Out-of-print. Available through EDRS. Call 1-800-227-ERIC.

ORDER FORM

Quantity   **Amount**

_____ Please begin my subscription to the 1989 *ASHE-ERIC
Higher Education Reports* at $80.00, 33% off the cover
price, starting with Report 1, 1989   _____

_____ Please begin my subscription to the 1990 *ASHE-ERIC
Higher Education Reports* at $80.00 starting with Report
1, 1990   _____

_____ Outside the U.S., add $10 per series for postage   _____

Individual reports are avilable at the following prices:

1988 and forward, $15	1983 and 1984, $7.50
1985 to 1987, $10	1982 and back, $6.50

*Book rate postage within the U.S. is included. Outside U.S., please add $1
per book for postage. Fast U.P.S. shipping is available within the U.S. at $1
per book; outside the U.S., $2.50 per book; orders over $50 may add 5%
of the invoice total. All orders under $25 must be prepaid.*

PLEASE SEND ME THE FOLLOWING REPORTS:

Quantity	Report No.	Year	Title	Amount

Subtotal:	
Postage(optional):	
Total Due:	

Please check one of the following:
☐ Check enclosed, payable to GWU-ERIC.
☐ Purchase order attached.
☐ Charge my credit card indicated below:
☐ Visa   ☐ MasterCard

Expiration Date _____

Name _____

Title _____

Institution _____

Address _____

City _____ State _____ Zip _____

Phone _____

Signature _____

SEND ALL ORDERS TO:
ASHE-ERIC Higher Education Reports
The George Washington University
One Dupont Circle, Suite 630
Washington, DC 20036-1183
Phone: (202) 296-2597